GOD WITH US;

OR, THE

PERSON AND WORK OF CHRIST,

WITH AN EXAMINATION OF

"THE VICARIOUS SACRIFICE"

OF DR. BUSHNELL.

BY

ALVAH HOVEY, D. D.,

PRESIDENT OF NEWTON THEOLOGICAL INSTITUTION.

Second Edition.

BOSTON:

GOULD AND LINCOLN,

59 WASHINGTON STREET.

NEW YORK: SHELDON AND COMPANY.

1872.

ROCKWELL & CHURCHILL, Printers, Boston.

PREFACE.

IN this the Golden Age of Periodicals and Fictions, a writer who ventures to address the reading public through a book, ought certainly to have good reasons for his course, and may be expected to give them, by way of preface to his work. I would therefore say, that the substance of what is here given on the Person and Work of Christ was laid before the readers of the "Examiner and Chronicle," a few years since, and that several of those readers expressed a desire to have the articles put into a more permanent form. The criticism of Dr. Bushnell's treatise on "The Vicarious Sacrifice" was written about six years ago, and has been read to a number of clergymen, as well as to several classes of students in the Newton

Theological Institution; whose wishes have been regarded in now committing it to the press. Though designed originally for publication, I have retained it in my own hands these many years, and revised it more than once, lest some of the language might seem to be unduly severe. But a further retention or revision of it promises no good result.

This little work is intended for the people. Knowing how rapidly they read and think in the present age, and how reluctantly they go through an exhaustive discussion of such themes as are treated in this volume, I have sought to state in brief yet popular language the decisive points of the controversy, and the obvious bearing of the Scriptures upon them. If it is too much to claim that every thought has been expressed with perfect clearness, it may at least be hoped that a constant aim to do this has rendered the style quite intelligible to every thoughtful reader. No one, therefore, has reason to turn from the book for fear that it will consume a large amount of time in the perusal, or that it will tax his powers of mind unduly. Yet, with this constant regard to brevity, clearness, and adaptation to the popular taste, has been united a strong desire to meet all the great difficulties which belong to the topics investigated. Results, if not processes, and processes when they seemed necessary to establish confidence in the results, have been given, and it is therefore believed that some who are in the high places of the field will find their faith confirmed, by looking again at the foundations on which it rests, by turning their eyes once more to the evidence that God has, in very deed, been with us on earth, and made expiation for the sins of the people.

But is not religious controversy unseemly and hurtful to piety? And will not the examination of "The Vicarious Sacrifice" be likely to do more evil than good? I am compelled to reply, that a certain amount of religious controversy is unavoidable. The friends of truth cannot and should not be altogether silent, when what they hold to be the truth is assailed, and what they believe to be error is maintained and extolled, even by men of distinction in the Christian ranks. Besides, both the precept and the example of Paul authorize the servants of Christ to contend earnestly for the faith once delivered to the saints.

But granting that religious controversy is sometimes unavoidable, are the views of Dr. Bushnell, as set forth in "The Vicarious Sacrifice," so defective as to require criticism at this late day? If I had not believed them to be extremely defective, and at the same time attractive, I should have given this criticism to the flames long ago; for I am conscious of no inward vocation to the office of censor. But the teaching of "The Vicarious Sacrifice," if defective, as I think, by denying any reaction of the Atonement upon the mind of God, is profoundly erroneous, and its influence must be even more hurtful, in many respects, than it would be if it embraced less truth and uttered it with less power.

If, then, the views of that work must be opposed,

ought it not to be done with exceptional kindness, on account of the eminent ability, worth, and devotion of its author? It should certainly be done with Christian forbearance and love, but also with fidelity to the Word of God. And if I have expressed a tithe of the indignation and scorn at the neology of that treatise which are poured out through it upon the doctrine of a really vicarious sacrifice on the part of Christ for the sins of the world, I have command of far stronger language than is commonly supposed, and ought to utter my convictions more tenderly. But the reader will discover no bitterness of spirit towards the distinguished author whose work is reviewed in the last part of this volume. It is the work only which is condemned, not the writer, to whom we are indebted for much true and inspiring thought.

With these explanations, the following pages are sent on their way, in the hope that He, whose Person and Sacrifice they are meant to honor, will make them a blessing to his people. "*Verily*,

verily, I say unto you, Before Abraham was, I am." "*Father, glorify thou me, with the glory which I had with thee before the world was.*" — Jesus Christ. "*The Word became flesh, and dwelt among us; and we beheld his glory, a glory as of the only begotten from the Father.*" — The disciple whom Jesus loved. "*Him who knew not sin, He made sin; that we might become the righteousness of God in Him.*" — The Apostle to the Gentiles.

A. H.

NEWTON CENTRE, Jan. 1, 1872.

CONTENTS.

PART FIRST.

THE PERSON OF CHRIST.

CHAPTER I.

THE DEITY OF CHRIST.

CHAPTER II.

THE HUMANITY OF CHRIST.

CHAPTER III.

THE UNITY OF CHRIST.

PART SECOND.

THE WORK OF CHRIST.

CHAPTER I.

THE ATONEMENT AS RELATED TO GOD.

CHAPTER II.

THE ATONEMENT AS RELATED TO MAN.

PART THIRD.

THE VICARIOUS SACRIFICE

OF DR. BUSHNELL.

CHAPTER I.

THE FUNDAMENTAL PRINCIPLES OF THE WORK.

CHAPTER II.

INTERPRETATION OF THE LANGUAGE OF SCRIPTURE

PART FIRST.

The Person of Christ.

GOD WITH US.

THE PERSON OF CHRIST.

INTRODUCTION.

THE religious thought of the present day is directed with unusual interest to the Person of Christ. Lives of Jesus are written, not so much, it would seem, to give a distinct picture of the events which marked his public course, and to make the reader familiar with the divine lessons which he taught, as to propound a theory of his nature and explain the secret of his power. Men study the record of his words for the purpose of finding some hint of the plan of his life, of the end which he meant to reach and the means which he chose for reaching it; or rather, it may be, for the purpose of obtaining support to a theory of his person which has already been formed in agreement with their favorite philosophy. Even writers of fiction are ready with an answer to the question, "What think ye of Christ? And in many instances their answer is one which the apostles would have promptly rejected, as coming from beneath, and not from above. Still it is given, and is read, and is received by many who are almost as ignorant of the Gospels as are the writers whom they admire. But this direction of thought to the person of Christ is not, on the whole, to be deplored. Much of the thinking may indeed be too bold, too speculative, too irreverent; it may be more eager to uproot Christian faith than to provide a substitute for it; it may lead astray some and perplex others; — but it shows the power of Christ in the world; it proves him to be the central character of history; it turns the eyes of mankind to him, the only true Light; and, under the wise direction of God, who makes the wrath of man praise him, it will result in honor to the Saviour and blessing to his church. The progress of truth will not be arrested. And even if some do not preach Christ at all, but only speak of him and call attention to him, this will not be wholly in vain; for their mistakes about his person will lead others to search the Scriptures anew and obtain clearer views of that person. We speak of *clearer* views advisedly; for the ideas which Christians have of their Lord may be substantially correct, and yet very indistinct. The truth may perhaps have been received by them, without deep and earnest study. They need therefore to examine it afresh and prove it, that they may hold it fast with a stronger faith. And to aid some of them, if possible, in this work, we propose to speak briefly of the Person of Christ, — of his deity and humanity, and of the union of these in his one personality.

CHAPTER I.

THE DEITY OF CHRIST.

I. HIS OWN TESTIMONY.

AS to the *deity* of Christ, it is natural for us to consult, in the first place, his own language. What did he say of himself? He spoke very plainly of his *pre-existence*, declaring that his life did not begin with his advent in the flesh. "No one has ascended up into heaven, but he that came down from heaven, the Son of man who is in heaven."[1] These words were addressed to Nicodemus, and were evidently intended to explain and justify what the Saviour had just been saying: "We speak what we know, and testify what we have seen. . . If I told you the earthly things, and ye believed not, how shall ye believe if I tell you the heavenly things?"[2] Equally explicit was his language at another time: "What then if ye see the Son of man ascend up where he was before?"[3] language which was used when his disciples murmured at the declaration: "I am the living bread

[1] John iii. 13. [2] John iii. 11, 12. [3] John vi. 62.

that came down from heaven. . . . He that eats my flesh and drinks my blood, has eternal life."[1] Moreover, in his last discourse with the eleven before his betrayal, he said to them: "I came forth from the Father, and have come into the world; again, I leave the world, and go to the Father;" and they responded: "Lo, now thou speakest plainly, and speakest no parable."[2] And, finally, in the prayer which he proceeded at that time to offer are the significant words: "And now, Father, glorify thou me with thine own self, with the glory which I had with thee before the world was."[3]

It is then perfectly plain that Christ was conscious of a heavenly existence prior to his earthly manifestation. But this is not all. There is one remarkable passage in the Gospel of John, which affirms, with the utmost precision and emphasis, his eternal existence. When the Jews, astonished and offended at his words, "Abraham, your father, rejoiced to see my day; and he saw it, and was glad," sharply and scornfully replied, "Thou art not yet fifty years old, and hast thou seen Abraham!"— Jesus said to them, "Verily, verily, I say unto you, BEFORE ABRAHAM WAS, I AM."[4] This language is much more exact and forcible in the Greek original than in the translation. The verb which is used of Abraham is not the same as the one which is used

[1] John vi. 51, 56. [2] John xvi. 28, 29. [3] John xvii. 5. [4] John viii. 56, 58.

of Christ. The former signifies an existence which has an origin, and it might be rendered, "came to be;" the latter denotes existence simply and absolutely, without any reference to origin. It is the timeless present, and by using it Christ claimed for himself the same eternal, unsuccessive, absolute being, which was claimed by Jehovah when he said to Moses: "I am that I am." It is not therefore surprising that the Jews, who refused to see in Christ anything more than a man, were full of wrath and took up stones to cast at him. It cannot be denied that they showed more respect for the honor of God, than do men at the present day who share their opinion of Christ, and yet, like Renan, eulogize his moral character. If he was not truly divine, he was profanely arrogant, or deplorably ignorant.

Jesus Christ also spoke of his *knowledge* as divine. A passage has already been quoted in which he claims to know the heavenly things, because he came down from heaven and is in heaven. No less clear and even more important are the words which he uttered in respect to his knowledge of God, the Father. "The Father loves the Son, and shows him all things that he himself does."[1] "All that the Father has are mine."[2]

[1] John v. 20. [2] John xvi. 15.

"It is my Father that honors me, of whom ye say that he is your God. And ye know him not, but I know him."[1] "No one knows the Son but the Father; nor does any one know the Father but the Son, and he to whom the Son is pleased to reveal him."[2] Surely this language is not that of a finite being. It claims a knowledge of God too intimate, direct and absolute to be natural in the lips of any being who was not conscious of a real oneness with the Father. It would of course be premature to attempt at this point a reconciliation of such language with the proper humanity of Christ; one thing at a time; and our purpose is now to show that his own words, naturally interpreted and received as true, prove his deity. This is all; and the sentences given above, if suffered to explain themselves by the light of the context in every instance, clearly show that Jesus thought himself to be possessed of divine knowledge. Indeed, his representation of himself as being in the past while in the present, — "before Abraham was, I am," — and as being in heaven while on earth,— "even the Son of man who is in heaven," — is a direct claim of being in his consciousness unlimited by time or space, and therefore an indirect claim of omniscience; for a person who is eternal and omnipresent must also be omniscient. A moment's

[1] John viii. 54, 55.

[2] Matt. xi. 27.

reflection will satisfy the reader of the truth of this statement, and will lead him to look upon the attributes of eternity, omnipresence and omniscience as in their very nature inseparable. Whoever possesses one of them must possess all of them.

Christ also spoke of himself as having divine *power*. For when accused of taking the place of God by pretending to forgive sins, he did not repel the charge nor explain away the force of his words; he did not suggest that the forgiveness of sins might be delegated by the Most High to another, or that he meant simply to declare what God had done; but he reasserted his unqualified power to forgive sins, by working a genuine miracle in the presence of his accusers. By the question, "Whether is it easier to say, Thy sins are forgiven; or to say, Arise and walk?"[1] he placed the power to forgive sins on a level with that to work miracles, and then vindicated his power to do the former by doing the latter. This is the most obvious meaning of the narrative; but on any reasonable view of it, Christ professed to work the miracle and forgive the sins himself. Nor is this all; he affirmed his essential oneness with the Father: "My sheep hear my voice, and I give to them eternal life; and they shall never perish, nor shall any one pluck them out of my hand. My Father, who has given them to me, is

[1] Matt. ix. 5.

greater than all; and no one is able to pluck them out of my Father's hand. I and my Father are one."[1] Here the Saviour declares his power to preserve his people, by asserting the omnipotence of the Father and his own oneness with him. Whatever power belongs to the Father belongs therefore to himself as well. Who can express the arrogance of such language in the mouth of a mere man? It can only be justified by supposing that the Good Shepherd who used it was truly God as well as man, and therefore, as to his essential nature, one with the Father, so that action apart from the Father was naturally impossible. Hence his words on another occasion: "My Father worketh hitherto, and I work;" and "what things soever he doeth, these also doeth the Son likewise."[2] And he goes on to say that he himself gives new life to those who are spiritually dead; that he will in the last day raise up from their graves those who are physically dead, and that he will judge all men, — the judgment being given to him by the Father, to the end that "all may honor the Son, as they honor the Father."[3] It is needless to urge the amazing force of this language, and the appalling vanity of any created being who could use it. According to his own words, the power of Christ was divine. If, however, any one thinks it pos-

[1] John x. 27-29. [2] John v. 17, 19. [3] John v. 23.

sible to understand his language as signifying only this, that God entrusted him with power and authority to work miracles, renew hearts, raise the dead, and judge the world, he may be answered in the words of Dr. South: "That God can no more give his power than his glory to another; there is no mortal arm can draw his bow." Or if the objection be modified, and it be urged that God acted at the word of Christ, it may be replied, first, in the words of Dr. Wardlaw, that "omnipotence placed at a creature's direction is indeed as real an impossibility in the divine administration as the endowing a creature with the attribute itself; for, in truth, if the attribute remains with God, it would amount to the very same thing as God's subjecting himself to his creature's . . . will;" and, secondly, that the language of Christ will not admit of such an interpretation. It claims for him divine honor as well as divine power.

Furthermore, Christ spoke of himself as an adequate *revelation* of the Father. Let this fact be deeply pondered. In the wonderful discourse recorded by John, he said to his disciples, "I am the way, the truth, and the life. No one comes to the Father, but by me. If ye knew me, ye would know my Father also; and from henceforth ye know him, and have seen him." Laying hold of this last expression, Philip interjected the remark,

"Lord, show us the Father, and it sufficeth us;" and Christ deliberately answered, "Am I so long time with you, and dost thou not know me, Philip? He that hath seen me hath seen the Father; and how sayest thou, Show us the Father?"[1] Surely this cannot be the language of one who deems himself a mere man! Too much is claimed and too calmly for such a view. To speak of himself as the way, the truth, and the life, is treading very closely on the holy ground which belongs to God; but to press on still further, and solemnly affirm, "He that hath seen me hath seen the Father," must be sacrilege in a merely human being. For it is well-nigh the strongest word that could be spoken. It is saying, "Whatsoever power, wisdom, holiness, love and mercy dwell in the bosom of God, and are the perfection of his nature, have been manifested in me. The fulness of the Godhead is in my person, and has been revealed to all who would see it by my life." But many other sayings of Christ agree with such a claim. For he puts his own presence with believers on a level with his Father's presence; he makes the Spirit's revelation of himself equivalent to his revelation of the Father; and by a variety of expressions he associates himself with the Father, as equal with equal. If, then, his own judgment of himself was correct,

[1] John xiv. 6, 7, 8, 9.

Jesus Christ, by virtue of his higher nature, was truly God. And if it was not correct, Christianity is a fable.

This is no exaggeration; for Christ made himself the centre of the religion which he taught. He declared himself to be the way and the truth, the resurrection and the life. He made trust or confidence in himself the one indispensable condition of access to God and fellowship with him, saying distinctly, "No man cometh unto the Father but by me."[1] "He that believeth on him, is not condemned; but he that believeth not, is condemned already, because he hath not believed in the name of the only begotten Son of God."[2] If Christ was mistaken at this point, if he did not understand his own person and work, the very core and heart of his religion is darkness. The foes of Christianity recognize this fact, and study, with zeal worthy of a better cause, to shake our confidence in the historical truth of the Gospels, in the moral perfection of Jesus, or in the crystal clearness of his self-knowledge. They see that if Christ was really what he claimed to be, according to the evangelists, pantheism and naturalism, the idols under which they worship self and sense, must inevitably fall, and the several doctrines of a personal God, of

[1] John xiv. 6.

[2] John iii. 18. Some interpreters suppose that these are the words of the evangelist, the discourse of Christ to Nicodemus ending with the 15th verse; but their view appears to be less probable than the one given above.

moral government, of human sinfulness, of divine revelation, of vicarious atonement, of a new birth, and of eternal judgment, must surely stand.

But it is becoming every day more evident that their assaults upon the historical truth of the Gospels will end in defeat, and the narratives of our Saviour's life hold their place as inspired records in the confidence of all good men. To those best qualified to judge, it is already evident that the furious and persistent attacks which have been made on the Gospels by modern sceptics will result, not only in a clearer understanding of their contents, but in a deeper reverence for their authority, so that unbelievers will be found to have served the cause which they assailed, and the Lord whom they despised. It is not, however, the purpose of this work to discuss the question of inspiration, but, resting with full assurance on the truth of God's word, to ascertain what may be known concerning the person of our blessed Lord. And from a brief examination of his recorded sayings, it has been shown that he claimed to be God,— to possess the attributes and exercise the prerogatives of a divine being.

This is no new conclusion. The followers of Christ, with few exceptions, have in every age interpreted his words in the same way. Devout and learned students of the Bible have so understood them. And the exposition which we have given is scarcely more than a repetition in other words of the deep and transparent language of the Master. He who knew the Father and himself, and who spake, as never man spake, with divine authority and clearness, has taught us what to think of his higher nature.

II. THE TESTIMONY OF HIS APOSTLES.

To present any just view of the evidence which the New Testament affords of the deity of Christ, we must add to his own words the testimony of his inspired apostles. For before leaving them, he declared that they were to bear witness of him, because they had been with him from the beginning; and at the same time he promised to send them, after his departure, the Spirit of Truth, to qualify them more perfectly for this service, by bringing to their remembrance his words, by giving them further knowledge of himself and his work, by revealing to them things to come, and by guiding them into all the truth. When thus endowed with the Spirit, and not before, they were to be Christ's witnesses in Jerusalem and in Judea and in Samaria, and unto the utmost part of the earth; and men who received them were to be looked upon as receiving him. Their doctrine was his doctrine; their preaching, the continuance of his preaching. In due time the promise of Christ was gloriously fulfilled; and, from the day of Pentecost onward, his apostles were animated with new faith and courage, with clearer views of his person and work, and with a cheerful purpose to shrink from no peril or toil in extending his spiritual reign. Such is a brief statement of the facts which authorize us to rely on their testimony respecting him as true. That testimony will deserve confidence as long as any part of the New Testament deserves it; for the doctrinal teaching of the apostles is inseparably and vitally connected with their historical teaching; both will stand or fall together; yea, they will stand forever; not one jot or tittle of them will fail.

But there is no one of the apostles to whom we more naturally look for instruction concerning the person of Christ than to John. For this disciple, whom Jesus loved, seems to have been endowed with qualities of mind and heart which drew him to the Saviour, and enabled him to appreciate, in a remarkable degree, his character. How, then, does he speak of his Master? He represents him as "the Word of Life," as "the Life which was manifested," and as "the eternal Life which was with the Father."[1] These are expressions which could

[1] 1 John i. 1, 2.

not have been applied by him to any man, however great or good. To think of calling Abraham or Moses "the Life," "the eternal life which was with the Father," is simply absurd. Again, he represents "the life" as "the light of men," "the light which shines in darkness," "the light of which John the Baptist was but a witness," and "the light which enlightens every man."[1] This language is much too strong to be used of a created being. To call any one "the light," in so pre-eminent a sense, is to pronounce him the original source of knowledge; and to call him "the Life" is to pronounce him the original source of spiritual good, — predicates which can be true of none but God. He, indeed, is light, and in him is no darkness at all; and he, too, is life, original, underived, boundless. But John is yet more explicit in the prologue to his Gospel, where he affirms of the higher nature of Christ, that it "was in the beginning with God," and indeed "was God."[2] The statement seems to be as free from ambiguity and obscurity as it could have been made. The deity of Christ is deliberately asserted, while at the same time his distinction from the Father is also asserted. Going back to the earliest event of which the human mind has any knowledge or conception, John declares that "In the beginning was the

[1] John i. 5, 7, 8, 9. [2] John i. 1.

Word;" so that his existence is dateless, eternal; when God created the heavens and the earth he was there. "And the Word was *with God*,"—the preposition here used signifying most intimate fellowship and love, and showing that "the face of the everlasting Word, if we may dare so to express ourselves, was ever *directed towards* the face of the everlasting Father." "And the Word *was* God,"—not a demigod, a being intermediate between deity and humanity, not an unimaginable something which separates the Infinite from the finite, the Creator from the creature; nor indeed, which is but another way of expressing the same thought, *a* god, a member of the family of gods; for John could not lapse for a moment into gnosticism or polytheism; but, simply and distinctly, God! *The Word was God.* This is the only interpretation which can be fairly given to the language of the apostle; and the most devout worshipper of Christ need not desire more exact or positive testimony to the fact of his Godhead.

Nor can we forbear to allude in this connection to another passage from the pen of the beloved disciple. At the close of his first letter, which was opened with testimony in respect to "the eternal life which was with the Father and was manifested to us," he says of himself and other Christians: "We are in the True One, in his Son, Jesus Christ.

This is the true God and eternal life." That is to say, we are in the true God, since, as ye very well know, we are in his Son Jesus Christ; and Jesus Christ is in fact, by virtue of his higher nature, the true God and eternal life. Thus interpreted, the statement of John is simple and logical, every clause adding an important thought to the foregoing, and the whole making complete sense; so that we are not required to apologize for the style of John in the words of Prof. Norton, who makes the last clause refer to God the Father: "Should it be said that these ideas are *not happily expressed*, I answer, it is evident that the author of this epistle was as *unskilful* a writer as we might expect to find one originally a Galilean fisherman."[1]

There is still another testimony of John which merits attention. After stating that, though Jesus had wrought so many signs before the Jews, they did not believe in him, he avers that the words of Isaiah the prophet were fulfilled by their unbelief, and then, having quoted the prophet's language concerning them, proceeds thus: "These things said Isaiah when he saw his glory and spoke of him."[2] According to the evangelist, the being whose glory Isaiah saw, was Christ; and the vision which he had of Christ's glory is described in the sixth chapter of his prophecies, and the being

[1] 1 John v. 20. [2] John xii. 41.

whose glory is there described is called Jehovah. He was sitting upon a throne, high and lifted up, and his train filled the temple. "Above it stood the seraphim, crying one to another, Holy, holy, holy is Jehovah of hosts; the whole earth is full of his glory." And this Jehovah is pronounced by the apostle John to have been Christ.

Nor is John the only apostle who identifies Jehovah, the God of his fathers, with Jesus Christ, the Saviour of men. Peter also, according to the true reading of a passage in his first Epistle, does the same. He exhorts his readers in the language of Isaiah: "Fear not with their fear, nor be troubled; but sanctify Christ as Lord in your hearts,"—translating the original "Jehovah of hosts" by the words "Lord Christ."[1] The first chapter in the Epistle to the Hebrews furnishes another instance of the same identification: "Thou, Lord, in the beginning didst lay the foundations of the earth, and the heavens are the works of thy hands,"[2] etc.,—words which are quoted from the one hundred and second psalm, a prayer addressed to Jehovah. Moreover, as the reader will not fail to observe, the extract from this psalm is given as the language of God the Father; doubtless because the sacred poet was conceived of as moved and assisted by the Spirit of God to compose the

[1] 1 Pet. iii. 15. [2] Heb. i. 10-12.

psalm, so that its words are indirectly, but in the deepest and most important sense, God's word. It will also be observed, that the paragraph cited in the Epistle to the Hebrews represents the Being who is addressed as the unchangeable Creator of all things; that this paragraph is introduced as language which was spoken to the Son, or in respect to him; and finally, that it is brought forward for the very purpose of establishing by divine testimony the proper sonship of Christ to the Father. It furnishes, therefore, indubitable evidence that the inspired writers of the New Testament identified the Saviour of men with Jehovah, the true God.

It will be unnecessary to go over all the apostolic testimony in support of the deity of Christ; but any discussion of the subject which makes no reference to the words of Paul must certainly be incomplete and unsatisfactory. What, then, does this great apostle say of his Master? It will be recollected that John, speaking of the Word who became flesh, declares that "All things were made by him, and without him was nothing made that has been made."[1] Paul affirms the same truth: "All things have been created by him and for him."[2] Creative power! Who of us has penetrated the mystery of this expression? It baffles

[1] John i. 3. [2] Col. i. 16.

our deepest thought. It signifies an unknown, incomprehensible force, doing that which to our reason is utterly impossible, yet absolutely necessary. We can perhaps imagine a power adequate to the support of the universe, but of a power which originates the lightest particle of matter we can form no conception whatever. It is too wonderful for us; and our last resort is to pronounce it almighty, and ascribe it to the infinite God. But this power is assigned by the apostle to Christ. And what is equally remarkable and conclusive, as evidence of the true Godhead of our Saviour, is the further statement that all things were made *for him*. He is at once the origin and the end of the creation. All things were made by him, as the supreme cause, and for him as the highest end. They were created for his glory, and will surely be made to manifest it, to magnify it; for his purpose cannot fail. But the apostle goes on in the same passage to say that "in him all things *consist*," — a deep and broad statement, according to which he is the strong One in whom the whole universe has its centre and unity, and by whom all its rolling masses and restless spirits are kept in being and in place. They stand together and form a cosmos in him. But this is not all. The same apostle associates "our Lord Jesus Christ" with "God the Father," as the primal source of grace, mercy, and peace to all believers,[1] and even characterizes the saints as those who "call upon the name of Jesus Christ our Lord,"[2] thus proving that true prayer, which must be regarded as an act of divine worship, was habitually offered to Christ by members of the primitive churches. This must be looked upon as cogent evidence in favor of his proper deity.

Besides all this, there are two passages in the letters of Paul which deserve particular attention, because they teach, in so many words, the deity of Christ. In one of them he urges the Philippian believers to have regard, not to their own, but to the things of others; and by so doing to have in themselves the mind which was also in Christ Jesus, "Who, being in the form of God, did not account it robbery to be equal with God; but emptied himself, taking the form of a servant, being made in the likeness of men."[3] It may perhaps be doubtful whether the apostle uses the expression "form of God" to signify his divine glory, or his divine condition, and whether he employs the word "robbery" to denote an unlawful act, or an object secured by such an act; but a decision of these points, in this way or that, does not affect the doctrinal import of his language. He plainly affirms that Jesus Christ, prior to his

[1] See, e.g., Gal. i. 3; Eph. i. 2. [2] 1 Cor. i. 2. [3] Phil. ii. 6 sq.

incarnation, was in the condition or glory of God; and that being thus, he looked upon his equality with God as something which rightfully belonged to him. This meaning of the apostle's words is made certain not only by their significance when viewed by themselves, but also by their relation to the context. "Worthless indeed would have been the example of Christ, had he been in reality a created being, who merely abstained from grasping at divine prerogatives which a creature could not have arrogated to himself without impious folly." All attempts to destroy the evidence which this passage gives in favor of the deity of Christ must prove to be futile.

In the other place referred to above, Paul, after enumerating several particulars in which the Israelites had been distinguished by the grace of God, adds finally, as their crowning distinction, "And of whom as to the flesh is Christ, who is over all, God blessed forever."[1] This is the only natural and proper version of the Greek original. No other rendering of the words would ever have been suggested, but for the perfect clearness with which, thus given, they teach the Godhead of Christ. A glance at the original text is enough to convince any competent scholar of this. And surely we are not at liberty to wrest

[1] Rom. ix. 5.

the apostle's language from its natural sense, in order to escape the conclusion that he looked upon Christ as God. To affirm, with Meyer, that Paul does not elsewhere speak of Christ as God, or as being over all, and therefore cannot be supposed to do so in this place, is certainly a mistake; for the apostle does speak of him elsewhere as One who was originally in the form of God, as One who did not deem it robbery to be equal with God, as One in whom dwelt all the fulness of the Godhead bodily,[1] and as One who is Head over all to the church. These statements are in obvious agreement with the passage now under consideration, and they remove all just grounds for the plea that he could not have described Christ as One who is over all, God blessed forever.

It would not be difficult to select many other passages from the New Testament which teach the deity of Christ; nor would it be difficult to prove that several prophecies of the Old Testament represent the Messiah as truly divine. But it is enough to have shown that the Saviour himself and his inspired apostles bear witness to this truth. If their witness is trustworthy, he was God; if it

[1] Col. ii. 9. "In whom *dwelleth* all the fulness of the Godhead bodily." If any one prefers to say that this language teaches the deity of the glorified Christ, and not of Christ in his humiliation, it will not affect the force of the passage as teaching the divinity of his higher nature. The word translated "Godhead" is the clearest and strongest possible, viz., θεότητος.

be not, Christianity is a fable; its founder and his authorized representatives were deceivers, and its peculiar doctrines worthless. This is not said for the sake of deterring any reader from the exercise of his own judgment upon the meaning and value of the New Testament. Far from it. Would that more attention were given to this precious volume! If the study of it were truly earnest, and thorough, and general, there would be less danger of mistaking its import at any vital point, and deeper reverence for its testimony to facts transcending our experience; difficulties would vanish, apparent contradictions would be reconciled, and the glory of Christ would be more wondrously revealed. But it is a fact only too evident, that many writers of the present day are making a thoroughly capricious use of the New Testament, rejecting whatever does not agree with their philosophy or feeling, and constructing from the broken sentences that remain an ideal Christ, utterly unlike the Son of God presented to us by the record in its integrity. In their hands Jesus of Nazareth is simply a good man; their principles of criticism require them to ignore all evidence which proves him divine. Against this arbitrary and unhistorical course we utter our protest.

The life of Jesus as a mere man will never be written; for the only authentic sources of knowledge respecting him assure us that he was not a mere man, that he did not act as such in his public ministry, that he was divine as well as human, in the past as well as in the present, in heaven as well as on earth, and that he taught as One having authority, not as the Scribes. And it cannot be amiss for us to gather up, now and then, as did our pious fathers, the certain evidence of his deity; observing, as we do it, how this evidence pervades the sacred narrative, as life does the human body, and reveals itself alike in what the Saviour said and in what he did not say, in what he did and in what he refused to do, giving to the record all its power and consistency. We hear its voice in his authoritative "*Verily, verily, I say* unto you," and in his mysterious "*I am* the way, the truth, the light, the resurrection, or the life." It is manifested to his glory by his speech and bearing in the exercise of miraculous power, by his predictions of coming to judge all men at the last day, by his response to the adjuration of the high priest, and by his language to Thomas after the emphatic confession of this disciple. It shines forth from the words of Peter which ascribe to Christ the outpouring of the Spirit at Pentecost; from the worship which primitive believers were accustomed to pay him in prayer; from the homage rendered him by the glorified in heaven, according to the testimony of John in the Apocalypse; and from the apostolic declarations which affirm this great truth. It is possible that the deity of Christ has sometimes been taught in such a way as to imply a disregard of his humanity; but if so, the reaction against this error has carried many to the other extreme; for they say little of his divinity, as if that was a matter of small account, while they dwell with delight on his humanity, as if that were enough to qualify him for all the work to be done in behalf of a sinful race. A greater mistake could not be made. We need a divine Redeemer; and Christ, who was divine, as well as human, is, let us hope, our Redeemer.

CHAPTER II.

THE HUMANITY OF CHRIST.

IN his able "History of the Doctrine of the Person of Christ," Professor Dorner shows that the early Christians were led to inquire respecting the elements of Christ's person, before they attempted to ascertain how these elements were united in him. And this is the natural order of investigation for all time; first, the facts, and then, if possible, the philosophy. For plainly it is needless to trouble ourselves about the union of two natures in Christ, until we know that he possessed two natures. Accordingly, having referred in the previous chapter to some of the evidence which requires us to believe in the deity of Christ, we now proceed to consider more briefly a part of the evidence for his humanity. More briefly; not because the human nature of Christ is a matter of small interest to us, for the salvation of men was dependent, so far as we can see, on his being truly man, but because it is now generally admitted that he was man. There have been times, no doubt, when believers in his deity thought too little and said too little of his humanity; but those times have passed quite away, and will not soon return. The writings of some who look upon his human nature as everything, have served a good purpose in directing attention to his moral excellence, to the nobility and strength and tenderness of his spirit, to the growth of his knowledge, the symmetry of his character, and the power of his example, and, in a word, to the qualities which belonged to him as man, and distinguished him as the perfect man. However blind to the signs of his higher nature, they have studied with enthusiasm and discussed with eloquence those of his lower. We may therefore treat them more briefly than would otherwise be desirable.

I. TESTIMONY OF CHRIST.

It is worthy of notice that Christ refers to himself once as a man: "Ye seek to kill me, a man who has spoken to you the truth."[1] And it cannot well be thought that this was done by way of accommodation to the belief of his hearers, without any regard to fact; for if he was not a man, as he seemed to be, and as he was supposed by them to be, he must have felt it his duty to shun every

[1] John viii. 40.

form of expression which would be likely to confirm their mistake. He could not, therefore, have called himself a man. To have done this deliberately, would have been to strengthen deliberately their belief in an error; to have done it thoughtlessly, would have been to forget himself, and to speak that which had no root or spring in his nature. It must, therefore, have been the truth which he uttered, and so whatever pertains to man as such, whatever is necessary to constitute one a complete human being, belonged to him. To deny this is to impeach his moral character; and to impeach his moral character is to impeach the historical truthfulness of the Gospels; and to do this is to trample on the plainest laws of evidence. For the existence of the Gospels can never be explained without the person and life of Christ. If they are not true, they are miracles of falsehood, more astonishing than any miracles of Jesus which they record. We beg the reader's pardon for using the word "if" in such a connection; and believe we may add, that, when called to defend the truthfulness of the Gospels, we feel very much as Paul felt when forced to defend his apostolic authority, being conscious of a sort of shame in commending that which is almost a part of our life, and which by its own excellence makes all words of commendation appear foolish. But to return from this digression; Christ called himself man, and this is conclusive evidence of his having a human nature.

No less expressive of his real humanity is the title, Son of man, which he so often applied to himself. For although this title is, in a certain sense, virtually given to the Messiah in the Old Testament,[1] it is but one of many there given to him, and is found in but a single passage; we cannot therefore suppose that it was preferred to all others by Jesus simply because it belonged to him as the Messiah. His habitual choice of it points to some other and special reason, — a reason to be sought in the designation itself. And this designation obviously signifies, not only that he had a human nature, but also that he had it from man, or by means of human parentage. It is not unfrequently used in the Old Testament as a synonyme for man. "God is not a man that he should lie, nor the son of man that he should repent." "How much less man that is a worm, and the son of man that is a worm." "What is man that thou art mindful of him, and the son of man that thou visitest him?" "In these, and similar passages," says an able writer, "son of man is obviously another name for one who is possessed of the attributes of humanity." This designation emphasizes the human origin and characteristics;

[1] Dan. vii. 13. The original reads: "One like a son of man."

it denotes one who is man by birth and nature; one who is a *born* man. Hence Christ was pleased to emphasize this double fact of his being man from man, by the name which he most frequently gave himself.

It is true that the Gospels speak of his virtually calling himself the Son of God about sixty times, by using the expression, My Father, with reference to God, and thus asserting, as the Jews rightly supposed, that God was his *own* Father, making himself equal in nature with God; but still more frequently, according to the same narratives, did he call himself the Son of man, making himself equal in nature with man. And even if we add to the former passages those in which he speaks of the Father absolutely, — as no one knoweth the Father but the Son, — they will not be found to outnumber the latter. Jesus Christ, then, was accustomed, for some reason, to denominate himself "the Son of man;" and, whatever his reason may have been, it is clear that the title which he chose to appropriate distinctly affirmed his humanity.

Moreover, he bore witness on the cross to the reality of his human body, by crying, "I thirst," and again after his resurrection, by saying, "A spirit hath not flesh and bones as ye see me have."[1] With equal clearness he attested the

[1] Luke xxiv. 39.

reality of his human spirit, by the pathetic words, "My soul is exceeding sorrowful, even unto death,"[1] and by the submissive language of his prayer, "Nevertheless, not as I will, but as thou wilt."[2] The longer one ponders this last expression, the more certain does it appear that Christ was capable of voluntary desires for that which he did not know it was the will of God to grant, and which, therefore, he would only ask in perfect submission to that will. And this assuredly proves that he had a finite spirit; for such desires must have been due to the motions, not of a divine and omniscient, but of a human and finite nature, and this nature must have comprised in itself a rational soul, capable of wishing for a definite good.

II. TESTIMONY OF THE SACRED WRITERS.

The inspired writers also assert the humanity of Christ. For they speak of him as man; they tell us of his mother and brothers and ancestors; they refer to his growth in wisdom and in stature, to his subjection to earthly parents, to his hunger, thirst, and weariness, and to a great number of events which give evidence of his proper humanity. They remind us that there is one Mediator between God and men, the man Christ Jesus; that he took part in

[1] Mark xiv. 34. [2] Mark xiv. 36.

flesh and blood, that he was made of a woman, made under the law, and indeed that he was made in all respects like his brethren. It is, however, unnecessary to present their testimony in full. The only point which we desire to emphasize is this, that whatever belonged to human nature as such, or in its normal state, belonged to Christ, *and was additional to his higher nature.* This point is one of vital importance, and needs to be urged at the present time. The eternal Word was not so changed as to be himself the human soul in the person of Jesus. No passage of the New Testament teaches such a doctrine, making Christ in his higher nature a humanized God, and in his lower nature a mere bodily organism. His human nature was complete, body, soul and spirit,[1] though mysteriously united with the divine. There is, in fact, just as good reason to believe that the Word was literally made a human body, as that he was made a human spirit. This statement could be verified by an examination of the sacred record; but such an examination would require too much space for these pages.

III. SINLESSNESS OF CHRIST'S HUMANITY.

The human nature of Christ was not only complete, it was also *sinless.* The narrative of his life

[1] This is not meant to be an endorsement of the theory that man's nature is "tripartite." Of that theory it is by no means necessary for the writer to express any opinion in the brief and practical treatment now attempted.

by the evangelists affords evidence of this fact; for the impression which, as a whole, it makes on the reader's mind, cannot in this respect be erroneous; and if we may trust that impression, he was a being without moral defect; he knew no sin, neither was guile found in his mouth. True, the perfection of his character has been called in question by some who have been trained to the higher (?) ethical standard of modern France, and who apologize for the defective morality of Jesus by charging it to the influence of his age and people; but they prepare the way for their assault upon his character, by rejecting the testimony of the Gospels, whenever it does not meet their views. Let that testimony throughout be received, and the sinless perfection of Christ will also be admitted. But this argument may be thought too summary and indefinite; we will therefore look at a few particulars.

Prof. Gess, of Basle, in his work on the Person of Christ,[1] makes use of the title, the Son of man, which was so often appropriated by Jesus, as a proof of his sinlessness. "According to the biblical view," he remarks, "sin is so utterly contrary to the original nature of man, that Jesus, by naming himself *the* Son of man, that is, the man who answers to the divine idea of man, either fell into

[1] The basis of Dr. Reubelt's work, entitled, "The Scripture Doctrine of the Person of Christ."

conflict with the sense of the whole Bible, or was conscious of being without sin." The strength of this argument depends of course upon the correctness of the view, that Jesus, by calling himself the Son of man, claimed to be, by way of distinction, the proper, normal man. The use of the definite article before Son is certainly significant; Jesus Christ did not profess to be simply *a* son of man, but rather *the* Son of man, standing, for some reason, pre-eminent and alone; and it is certainly natural to suppose that he thus isolated himself, because in him alone was realized the true idea of man; in all others it was obscured by sin. But however this may be, Christ did, beyond question, lay claim to sinless perfection. For he said, "My meat is to do the will of Him that sent me;"[1] and what stronger language could he have found to express his absolute satisfaction in doing the will of God? And again, "The Son can do nothing of himself, but what he seeth the Father do;"[2] "I and my Father are one;" "He that hath seen me hath seen the Father." How could the Saviour have taught more positively the perfect agreement of his own character and action with those of God? Or again, "The Father loveth the Son, and showeth him all things that he himself doeth."[3] Was this love, thus expressed, bestowed on a sinful being? And

[1] John iv. 34. [2] John v. 19. [3] John v. 20.

let it not be said that the word Son, as used in these passages, refers exclusively to the higher nature of Christ, and therefore such language proves nothing in respect to the sinlessness of his human nature. For the language used by Jesus was intended to explain or justify his conduct, and the word Son must therefore have referred to himself as a person. But the person of Christ was one, embracing his lower nature as well as his higher, and there is no reason to suppose any moral discord between these two natures in him.

But there is another expression which merits deep consideration, and must be interpreted of the entire person of Christ. On a certain occasion he said to the Jews, "Which of you convinceth me of sin?"[1] And this challenge is equivalent to an assertion of his sinless perfection. For he had just declared that "Whosoever committeth sin is the servant of sin," meaning evidently that a single act of sin presupposes the actor to be in a state and habit of sinning, or under law to sin, so that he is unworthy of absolute confidence; while in the clause which follows the challenge cited he goes on to say, "But if I speak the truth, why do ye not hear me?" That is, he argues from the fact of his sinlessness to the absolute truth of his teaching, and from this to the duty of his hearers to believe

[1] John viii. 46.

him. The word translated "sin" retains its usual signification in this place, and the meaning of our Saviour's question is obvious to the careful reader. With this passage may be joined another, in which Christ says of the Father, "I do always the things that please him;" [1] for an activity which is perpetual, and ever in exact agreement with the will of God, must spring from a holy source.

There is still another passage worthy of attention, namely, "The prince of this world cometh, and in me hath nothing." [2] Luthardt appears to have caught the true sense of these words. "Christ names him the prince of this world, because, in so far as the world is estranged from God, it is under his sway. For he rules in all that is hostile to God, in sin and death. . . But it is also true, 'in me he hath nothing.' Jesus indeed is in the world, and so in the domain of the Wicked One: but he is not of the world; hence there is nothing in Jesus to which the Wicked One could cling; in Jesus he has nothing which is his, which can be said to belong to him, upon which or from which he could establish a claim on Jesus. This is the simplest explanation of the clause." And thus interpreted, the language of Christ embraces a denial of his sinfulness. Augustine understood it to make this exclusively, "nothing in me" signify-

[1] John viii. 29. [2] John xiv. 30.

ing, as he thought, "no sin at all in me;" and Alford pronounces this to be the only right interpretation, adding, however, for himself, "no point of appliance whereon to fasten his attack."

Turning now from the testimony of Christ to that of inspired men, we read in the first Epistle of John as follows: "Ye know that he was manifested to take away our sins; and in him is no sin;" and "He that doeth righteousness is righteous, even as he is righteous."[1] Paul also teaches that "he made him to be sin, *who knew no sin*, that we might become the righteousness of God in him;"[2] and the writer of the Epistle to the Hebrews avers that Christ "through the eternal Spirit offered himself *without spot* unto God."[3] Such proof of the actual sinlessness of Christ is conclusive.

And the total impression made by the record of his life affords evidence of the same fact; a kind of evidence which cannot easily be overrated. For it does not depend upon minute points of criticism which only a scholar can understand, but upon the broader features and general tone of the narrative which can be appreciated by every upright mind. The eye of an unlearned but thoughtful reader is almost sure to take in the great features of the picture, and judge them correctly. To borrow an illustration, the microscopic eye of the scholar is

[1] 1 John iii. 5, 7. [2] 2 Cor. v. 21. [3] Heb. ix. 14, cf. vii. 26.

often less useful in this respect than the unaided eye of the common reader. Yet unbelievers are not wholly insensible to the general effect of the gospel narratives; though they sadly mar that effect by rejecting what they please as false.

Says one of this class: "Humanity, as a whole, presents an assemblage of beings, low, selfish, superior to the animal only in this, that their selfishness is more premeditated. But in the midst of this uniform vulgarity, pillars rise towards heaven and attest a more noble destiny. Jesus is the highest of these pillars, which show to man whence he came and whither he should tend. In him is condensed all that is good and lofty in our nature. He was not sinless; he conquered the same passions which we combat; no angel of God comforted him, save his good conscience; no Satan tempted him, save that which each bears in his heart. And, as many of the grand aspects of his character are lost to us by the fault of his disciples, it is probable also that many of his faults have been dissembled. But never has any man made the interests of humanity predominate over the littleness of self-love so much as he. Devoted, without reserve, to his idea, he subordinated everything to it to such a degree that towards the end of his life the universe no longer existed for him. It was by this flood of heroic will that he conquered heaven. . . He lived only for his Father, and for the divine mission which he believed it was his to fulfil. . . Whatever may be the surprises of the future, Jesus will never be surpassed. His worship will grow young without ceasing; his legend will call forth tears without end; his sufferings will melt the noblest hearts; all ages will pronounce, that, among the sons of men, there is none born greater than Jesus." With such language does Renan close his fiction entitled "The Life of Jesus," — language which is bold, positive, vivacious, flippant, but which is inconsistent, conceding either too much or too little. If Jesus had the moral defects of which he is accused by Renan, he was the most arrogant and blasphemous of men, and in the end will be so regarded. Ignorant of himself, and conniving at deception, he was at best a blind enthusiast, more to be pitied than to be revered, more to be admired that to be respected. But he was in reality free from those defects, and the eulogy of Renan does not approach the excellence of a true description of his character as delivered by the Gospels.

But how was it that he escaped the contamination of moral evil? This question is answered by the words of the angel to Mary: "The Holy Spirit will come upon thee, and the power of the Highest will overshadow thee; therefore also the Holy One that is born shall be called the Son of God."[1] By the action of the Holy Spirit at his supernatural conception, depravity was excluded from the human nature of Jesus, and he came into the world at birth as upright as Adam before the fall. As to the original and essential qualities of human nature, it behooved him to be made in all respects like his brethren; but as to sin and a bias to sin, it was proper that he should differ from them and fulfil all righteousness. His infirmities were natural, not moral. His susceptibilities of body and spirit were thoroughly human, but not depraved. He could feel the attractions of power, of honor, of repose, and the pangs of hunger and thirst and bereavement; but his love of right was always supreme, and his submission to the will of God perfect. Such was Christ as a man, holy, harmless, undefiled, from first to last without sin, the model man, giving us an example of what the race might have been had our first parents been steadfast in virtue, and of what the Christian should aim to become by the aid of divine grace.

[1] Luke i. 35.

CHAPTER III.

THE UNITY OF CHRIST'S PERSON.

HAVING shown that Jesus Christ was both God and man, it remains for us to notice briefly the evidence afforded by the Scriptures that he was but *one person*, and to explain as well as possible the meaning of this expression when applied to him. As to the evidence in question, a brief notice must suffice, because the fact which it establishes is now freely admitted by the great body of Christians, and because an attempt to define or explain the fact will require all the space which can be given to this topic.

The proof contained in the Gospels that Christ was but a single personality is abundant. Almost every page of the narrative may be said to teach this fact. For generally, if not always, Christ used a singular pronoun in speaking of himself. Thus, "I say unto you;" "I am the Good Shepherd;" "I am the true vine;" "If ye love me, keep my commandments;" "He that receiveth you receiveth me;" "Whosoever shall confess me before men, him will I also confess before my Father who is in heaven;" and many other expressions of the same kind. Very rarely, if ever, did he use the plural form of the pronoun when referring to himself alone. Possibly, in John iii. 11; yet it is far more likely that Jesus referred to his disciples, along with himself, in this place. The best expositors understand him to do this, and the view gives especial point to his language in reply to Nicodemus. Yet this form was often chosen by the apostle to the Gentiles, and, according to the Old Testament, it was sometimes employed by God himself. But, while giving evidence in many ways of possessing divine as well as human attributes, Christ felt it necessary to guard his followers against the error of denying the unity of his person. And this he seems to have done by always referring to himself in the singular number, and by speaking as though he was a single being.

If any one is ready to call in question this view of his motive, and to say that he spoke thus solely because it was natural for him to do so, because such was the spontaneous expression of his consciousness, we need not stop to debate the point; for the objection fully admits that his personal consciousness was a unit, and requires us to conceive of him, not as two beings existing side by side and acting together as one, for the attainment of a common end, but as a single person in whom deity and humanity were united. And if further evidence be required, we may refer to the fact that the union of the divine and human natures in Christ was effected at his conception, at the moment when the Holy Ghost came upon the Virgin Mary, and the power of the Highest overshadowed her. Hence the child Jesus was holy at birth, and was from the first the Son of God and the Son of man. This is the obvious meaning of the sacred narrative. It points directly to a personal union of the higher and the lower natures of Christ. It forbids us to suppose that he was no more than one of the ancient prophets, with whom the Spirit of God clothed himself as with a garment.[1]

Turning now to a more difficult task, we must try to define the expression, "one person," as applied to Christ. What does it mean? How was his divine nature related to the human, and his human nature to the divine? How far is it possible for us, instructed by our own experience, and the holy Gospels, to explore the realm of his personality and consciousness? That we may look into that realm and behold some of its wonders is certain; but it is also certain that much of it lies beyond the utmost reach of our vision. "Great is the mystery of godliness." The reader may therefore be sure beforehand that many questions

[1] See Judges vi. 34; 1 Chron. xii. 18.

of deep interest will be left unanswered, even if he is not forced to exclaim as we proceed, "Who is this that darkeneth counsel by words without knowledge?" Why, then, attempt a definition or explanation of the kind proposed? Because it is desirable to fix certain "metes and bounds" to the sense of words used by us. If this cannot be done in the present instance,—if no account whatever can be given of the expression, "one person,"—it would be just as well to say one mystery. Besides, if our attempt fails to set the truth in clearer light, it will at least be a protest against views which we reject as erroneous. But it may not be rash to hope that the truth itself can be more fully and exactly stated than it is by the single expression, "one person."

I. THEORY THAT CHRIST HAD NO HUMAN SOUL, BUT THE LOGOS.

Unity of consciousness is involved in unity of person. Now it is easy to see that if Christ had but one spiritual nature (the eternal Word) his consciousness might be single. But in that case his humanity would be imperfect, consisting of a body only, without any soul; and the language of Scripture is incompatible with such a view of his human nature. He was a complete man, and as such possessed a human spirit. To meet this difficulty, it has been often said of late that the eternal Word reduced himself to the measure and state of a human soul when it comes into being; that he awoke to conscious life, grew in knowledge and power, and experienced weakness, ignorance, and trial, as a mere man, — in a word, that from being truly divine he became truly human. This view has many conspicuous advocates in Germany, and a few in America. In their opinion it not only provides for the unity of Christ's person, but also represents God as coming into the closest imaginable fellowship and sympathy with man. For he makes himself literally one of us, and learns by experience our infirmities. Among the advocates of this theory must be numbered the Rev. Henry Ward Beecher, both in printed sermons and in "The Life of Jesus the Christ." From the latter a few sentences may properly be quoted: "Christ was very God. Yet, when clothed with a human body, and made subject to physical laws, he was then a man, of the same moral faculties as man, of the same mental nature, subject to precisely the same trials and temptations, only without the weakness of sin. A human soul is not something other and different from the divine soul. It is as like it as the son is like his father. God is father, man is son. As God in our place becomes human, — such being the similarity of the essential natures, —

so man in God becomes divine. Thus we learn not only to what our manhood is coming, but when the Divine Spirit takes our whole condition upon himself, we see the thoughts, the feelings, and, if we may so say, the private and domestic inclinations of God. . . Manhood is nearer to godhood than we are wont to believe." Again: "Who shall say that God cannot put himself into finite conditions? Though as a free spirit God cannot grow, yet as fettered in the flesh he may. Breaking out at times with amazing power, in single directions, yet at other times feeling the mist of humanity resting upon his eyes, he declares, "Of that day and that hour knoweth no man, no, not the angels which are in heaven, *neither the Son*, but the Father." (Chap. III.) The same theory has found more learned, if not more eloquent advocates in Germany, the fatherland of speculative theology for modern times, and certain expressions of the New Testament have been employed with no little skill in commending it to the favor of Christians. Especially has it been urged by the leading defenders of this view, that John, in his Gospel, speaks of the Word as having become, not "man," but "flesh," and declares, in his first Epistle, that "every one who confesseth that Jesus Christ has come in flesh is of God," while Paul affirms that "in him dwelleth all the fulness of the Godhead bodily."

These arguments from the letter of Scripture are not, however, deemed conclusive by any eminent expositor, and therefore stress is also laid on the simplicity and clearness of the doctrine itself.

But there are fatal objections to this theory. For it supposes the place of one person of the Holy Trinity to be vacated for a time. It supposes the infinite attributes of the Word to be made latent by the incarnation, and the divine, *as such*, to have no experience of the human, for it ceases to be divine by becoming human. Hence this theory fails at the very point where it deems itself strongest. For if we cannot understand how two natures, one infinite and the other finite, can be comprehended in the action of a single consciousness, it is surely impossible for us to understand how the consciousness of the eternal Word can be one and unbroken, while the infinite becomes finite and again the finite infinite. If God, in whose mind there is no succession, cannot become consciously one with a human being existing in time, he cannot be one with the Word made finite and existing in time. The transition from the one mode of existence to the other must break the tie of consciousness. When the divine experience ceases the human begins, and when the human ceases the divine begins, otherwise there must be two modes of experience, two consciousnesses at the same instant.

It is surely as difficult to believe that one consciousness embraces at the same moment both the finite and the infinite experience of a single spiritual nature, — the experience belonging to two different modes and periods of existence, — as it is to believe that one consciousness embraces, at the same time, the action of two spiritual natures, one finite and the other infinite. Hence nothing is really gained by this view, which supposes Christ to have been God, *minus* actual deity, and man, *minus* a real human spirit. The divine is not brought nearer to the human; for the human experience is not carried up into the divine state and consciousness, unless at the sacrifice of all, and more than all, that is supposed to be gained by the theory. Besides, if the doctrine of Mr. Beecher is true, there must be, in the other world, Lords many and Gods many; for, as the Divine Spirit becomes human by taking on a human body, so human spirits become divine by laying aside the flesh. In other words, the limitations of the human spirit are not at all due to its own nature, but wholly to its connection with the body. Must it not then follow, either that the human and finite mode of existence is better than the divine and infinite, of which the spirit of man is in itself capable; or, else, that the apostles were foolish in their joy at the prospect of a resurrection; or, finally, that the glorified bodies of saints are ubiquitous; bringing us back to the doctrine of Lords many and Gods many, and admitting that M. Comte was more than half right, when he pronounced men, or at least women, to be the Supreme Being? In fact, there are not many graver errors in the world of thought than the one which is so warmly and positively taught by Mr. Beecher, namely, that the creature and the Creator, the human spirit and its Author, are one in kind, and only different in degree, through the limitations of the body.

It may also be remarked, that the title, "Son of man," so often applied to himself by Christ, naturally signifies one whose human nature was derived from man, *man from man;* not one the more important part of whose human nature was from God, and in essence was God. But the force of this expression has been given in speaking of the Humanity of Christ, and therefore need only be referred to in this place.

It will be observed that Dr. Crosby emphasizes the word *became* in John i. 14, and gives to the word "flesh" the sense, "man," or "human;" while Mr. Beecher lays all the stress upon the word "flesh," supposing the expression to signify that "the Divine Spirit (?) had enveloped himself with the human body, and in that condition been subject to the indispensable limitations of material laws."

The former misinterprets the verb, and the latter the noun. The word "flesh" signifies in this passage, as also in others where birth is referred to, human nature, and especially human nature as distinct from the divine. The reader will not fail to note the use of the same word in the preceding verse, and again in John iii. 6: "That which is born of flesh is flesh." He will also notice the same verb in Gal. iv. 4, where the Son of God is said to have been "made of a woman."

Moreover, the theory in question is condemned by the obvious meaning of Christ's language on several occasions. "Neither knoweth any one the Father, save the Son;" "The Son of man hath power on earth to forgive sins;" "The Son of man who is in heaven;" "Before Abraham was I am;" "My Father worketh hitherto, and I work;" "What things soever he doeth, these also doeth the Son likewise;" "As the Father raiseth up the dead and quickeneth them, even so the Son quickeneth whom he will;" "As the Father hath life in himself, so hath he given to the Son to have life in himself."[1] On this last passage Prof. Gess, an able advocate of the view under consideration, remarks, "Did not the Son, then, possess the life of God while on earth as well as in his pre-existent state? If this word

[1] John v. 26.

of Jesus refers to his earthly life no less than to that which preceded and followed it, we must answer this question in the affirmative; and then all that we have said in respect to the self-exinanition of the Logos in becoming flesh would be overthrown." The Christian reader will not fail to study the "word of Jesus," and this study will convince him that it refers to the incarnate Logos. It is also worthy of notice that one of the passages which are alleged in support of this theory, namely, "the Word was made flesh," if it proves anything on the point, proves much more than is believed by those who appeal to it; for it affirms that the Word was made human flesh, a human body, just as clearly as it affirms that he was made a human spirit. But it affirms neither, in the sense supposed.

II. THEORY THAT CHRIST HAD VIRTUALLY TWO HUMAN SOULS.

Equally unsatisfactory is another view which has many advocates at the present day. It agrees with the one just rejected in asserting that the Word who was God became truly human, but differs from it by teaching that Jesus Christ had a genuine human soul, in addition to the humanized Word. Accordingly, there were in him two homogeneous, spiritual natures, both on probation and exposed to trial, yet sinless, both finite in experience and subject to the law of growth in knowledge and virtue; but one of them possessing unconsciously all the perfections of God, while the other had no attributes but those originally given to man. It is true that this theory avoids the error of supposing Christ to be neither God nor man, in the fullest sense of these terms, but only God *minus* deity and man *minus* spirit; yet it does not escape the error of affirming an incredible change in the Godhead, and of disregarding the plain meaning of Scripture. Everything which was urged above against the former theory presses with equal force against the one now under consideration; while the chief reason for adopting that theory, namely, that it enables us to conceive distinctly of Christ as one person, cannot be used in support of this. For the personal union of two finite spirits is just as incomprehensible as such a union of an infinite spirit with a finite. But if this were not so, the difficulty would remain; for in his present state of glory, Christ, though retaining his human nature, is admitted by those who maintain this theory to have in exercise all the attributes of God; and if a personal union of the infinite Word with a human spirit in glory is possible, such a union may certainly be possible on earth; for the gulf between the infinite and the finite can never be filled by any growth of the latter. It is therefore necessary to believe that the human nature of Christ has been endowed with powers strictly divine, that is to say, has been literally deified, or to believe that the Lamb in the midst of the throne is now both infinite and finite in one person.

The Lutheran doctrine of the Real Presence in the Elements of the Lord's Supper, implying, as it does, the ubiquity of Christ's glorified human nature, has had a powerful influence in leading German theologians to adopt the former alternative. And a belief that the human has been transmuted into the divine has doubtless favored a belief that the divine was made human, in the person of Christ on earth. But reasonably interpreted, the Word of God does not, we think, authorize either of these beliefs. It neither teaches that the second person of the adorable Trinity emptied himself of his divine consciousness and power, nor that man will ever cease to be finite. And surely the difficulties of the incarnation, for human reason, are not at all diminished, by supposing that God was converted into man in order to effect a personal union with our nature. We must therefore reject this theory also.

III. THEORY THAT CHRIST'S CONSCIOUSNESS EMBRACED THE ACTION OF BOTH DIVINE AND HUMAN FACULTIES.

What then is the true view? In what sense was Christ, though God and man, one person, the God-man? In the same sense, we believe, that any man, as a unity composed of body and spirit, is one person. His consciousness was single, though it embraced the motions of two most unequal natures, the one divine and the other human; so that whatever could be affirmed of either nature could be affirmed of him. He was independent of space and time, omnipresent, omniscient, almighty; but he was also limited, by space and time, in knowledge and in power. By virtue of the divine side of his person, the former was true of him; and by virtue of the human side, the latter. This view has the merit of being at once natural and obvious. It supposes the divine to be always truly divine, and the human to be truly human. It agrees with the plain and full sense of biblical language. And it is partially illustrated by the personal union of soul and body in man. This illustration is the only one which can be said to cast a ray of light upon the treatment of our subject in the Word of God, and it deserves careful attention.

Let it then be observed that, to human reason,

the difference between body and soul, matter and spirit, is so utter and complete, that a personal union between the two is just as inconceivable as such a union between man and God, the finite and the infinite. This language is not extravagant; in our judgment it is literally correct. Had we no experience of the former union, it would require quite as much faith to believe it possible as it does to believe the latter possible. For the reason of man is utterly baffled when it tries to pierce the mystery of any connection whatever between matter and spirit. Impact or influence of one upon the other is inconceivable. Yet the fact of connection, of interdependence, and of personal unity, is certain. There is therefore, in reality, no solid ground on which we can stand in denying the union of deity and humanity in the person of Christ. Let it also be observed that we say of a man, he thinks, feels, wills, loves, hates, hopes, fears; and, with equal propriety, he is hungry, thirsty, muscular, frail, black, white, and the like. Whatever is true of his mind or of his body is true of the man in whom these are personally united. For his consciousness claims for him the motions and affections belonging to both elements of his nature. Pain of limb and sorrow of soul are not the same in character or source; one is recognized as having its seat in a material organ, and the other in an immaterial principle; yet both are taken up into the consciousness, and by this mediating and uniting power, elements the most diverse, body and spirit, are made to suffer with each other. Wonderful indeed is the sympathy between them, but more wonderful the action of consciousness in binding together such opposites in one personality. And this is the only kind of personal existence known by experience to those addressed by the Word of God.

In the light of this analogy we turn to the Sacred Record, and find no difficulty in believing that Jesus Christ while on earth was the God-man; that his personal being comprehended three elements, instead of one or two; that he was conscious of trial, of weakness, of growth in knowledge, of virtue confirmed by obedience; and that his divine nature suffered in a peculiar manner with the human, while on the other hand his human nature often received special light and strength from the divine. By virtue of his human nature he possessed and uttered the thoughts, feelings, desires, and appetites of man, — these desires being never inordinate or tyrannical, but always in subjection to the will of God; and by virtue of his divine nature he had, and at times expressed, the wisdom, power, and authority of God. How could he do otherwise, and hope to be understood by men? He must predicate of himself all which his consciousness claimed for him as a person; and since the range of elements in his being was the widest conceivable, the contents and the utterances of his consciousness must have the widest range conceivable. Bearing this in mind, the language of Christ, as recorded in the Gospels, will be found, for the most part, perfectly natural and intelligible.

"For the most part," we say, because there is at least one passage with which the view now given does not seem to agree; namely (Mark xiii. 32), "Of that day or hour no one knows, not even the angels in heaven, nor the Son, but the Father;" and this language appears at first sight to deny that Christ knew in any sense, even in his higher nature, the time of the last day. But what if Jesus, acting as Mediator between God and men, must apprehend by the faculties of his human soul, as well as by his higher nature, whatever he taught? And what if the powers of his human soul, though strengthened by the grace of the Holy Spirit given without measure, had thus far been in quest of more profitable truth, and had not so much as craved a knowledge of the date in question? So that speaking, as he ever did, in his mediatorial capacity, Christ had not a knowledge of that hour? It is surely conceivable that such was the law of his action, and that, while the fact of his higher nature being truly God, and therefore omniscient, was revealed to the faculties of his human soul, and could therefore be affirmed by him as a theanthropic being, the particulars of that omniscience were only apprehended by his human faculties in part, even as they were needed for his Messianic work. In a certain sense, to be sure, his knowledge was unrestricted, infinite, — even as Peter felt when he exclaimed, "Lord, thou knowest all things, thou knowest that I love thee;" and as Christ was assured when he said, "The Father loveth the Son, and showeth to him all things which he himself doeth." His higher nature was omniscient, but the lower was not. Yet even this, the lower, was never, it may be confidently affirmed, in ignorance of what pertained to the work of any hour or moment of the Saviour's life. The divine was ever in communication with the human, giving it light for every emergency; and the human was ever absorbed in its proper work, untroubled about curious questions or events in the distant future. All its powers were taxed to the utmost in doing well the vast work of the present. Let me use an illustration.

The storehouse of knowledge in the human mind is called memory; the power by which any portion of that knowledge is taken up and set before the eye of consciousness is called recollection. Now every man is sure that he has vast treasures of fact and thought in his memory, which are not at any one moment in his recollection or consciousness; yet many of them are at least within calling distance, and can be summoned into the consciousness by circumstances and needs, if not otherwise. They are in the vast penumbra which encompasses the orb of consciousness, and can be drawn from twilight into day by the cry of the soul. They come at the beck of circumstances, and do their work, but again retire when the eye of attention is satisfied. It will be seen that the power of recollection or attention is limited to a much smaller circle than that of memory. The former cannot take in at once all the stores of the latter; yet, in a perfect state of the mind, it may conceivably have *command* of them all, and be able to use them one by one. So all the treasures of knowledge in the divine nature of Christ were, it may be said, at the service of his human nature, and would answer its call in every hour and need of the Messianic work. But there would be no call and no need, in that work, of knowledge in respect to the day and hour of the end. And therefore, speaking as the God-man, engaged in his mediatorial work, Christ could say, "Neither the Son, but the Father." Possibly another illustration may aid the reader to our meaning. The action of the human faculties of Jesus may be compared to a small sphere of colored light in the centre of an infinite sphere of white light, with such a connection between the two that they are not only identical through the full extent of the smaller sphere, but the light of the larger sphere is ever within reach of the smaller and felt to be virtually its own for all mediatorial service.

This, then, is our view of the Saviour's Person. He was the God-man, truly divine and truly human, his single consciousness embracing, in some mysterious way, the action of both natures, the infinite and the finite. And by the aid of such a view all the language of the Scriptures on the subject before us may, we think, be readily understood.

IV. THE TEMPTATION OF CHRIST NO OBJECTION TO THIS THEORY.

No view of the Saviour's person which disagrees with the recorded facts of his experience can be correct. And among the most remarkable facts of that experience may be reckoned the instances of temptation which are related in the Gospels, and referred to in the Epistle to the Hebrews. If it can be shown that what the Saviour felt, when he was "tempted of the devil," was inconsistent with the view of his person already given, that view must, of course, be rejected. But the reader will be kind enough to mark our language. We do not say that a correct view of the person of Christ must be exhaustive, enabling us to *comprehend* his temptation, to see *how* it was possible; for we can hope to comprehend but little in the present life; we see through a glass darkly; and there were mysteries in the being of Christ, as there are in the being of every Christian, which no human vision can pierce. A view may be correct, as far as it goes, which leaves many a question unanswered, many a secret unexplored; but a view which is demonstrably inconsistent with known facts must be incorrect. Can it, then, be shown that the sinlessness of Christ's human nature, or its personal union with his divine nature, still acting as divine, is incompatible with the fact of temptation to evil? We think not, but must answer each part of the question by itself.

To the first part we reply, that temptation to evil may be experienced by a being who is not morally depraved. The existence of sin is proof enough of this; for it cannot be maintained that God created moral beings with an original bias to evil. Wherever, then, in the universe, sin exists, it must be due to the action of beings who were made upright. But to say that upright beings have sinned, is to say that they were susceptible of enticements to sin, and this is as much as to say that they could be tempted to evil. So it was with our first parents in Eden. They were created in the image of God. Their spiritual powers and inclinations were all right. But the tempter came, appealing to those principles of their nature which might be warmed, heated, inflamed into pride, ambition, selfish desire, appetite, and they fell sheer down into the abyss of sin and death. It may and must be a mystery to us how the lies of Satan entered into the less spiritual susceptibilities of their nature, and stimulated them to abnormal and controlling action; but somehow it was done; the progenitors of our race, though morally perfect, were tempted to evil, and promptly yielded to the seductive influence. This great fact is replete with instruction, applicable to the question before us. Indeed, it may be said to furnish a satisfactory answer to that question.

But while this will be readily admitted, it may perhaps be urged that Christ was tempted *in all points* like as we are, and therefore must have had a human nature in the same moral condition as ours. To this we reply: The biblical statement that he was tempted in all points like as we are, is qualified by the words, "without sin;" and it is impossible to show that these words refer exclusively to the peculiar result of temptation in his case, and not also to his spiritual purity as modifying its hold upon him. The interpretation which Dr. Moll gives to this limiting clause is in our judgment correct: "The common explanation — namely, without his temptation leading him to sin — is too narrow. The participation of Jesus in every form of human suffering; the actual stirring of his emotions, his complete fellow-feeling with our weakness, the reality of his actual temptation,— all have taken place without one single sinful emotion, and without even finding in him, as their condition or point of contact, a single slumbering element of sin. Everything took place with him 'separately from sin.'" This is doubtless a correct exegesis of the words; and, if so, the sacred writer has cautioned us against supposing that the sinless humanity of Christ felt the power of temptation *just as* it is felt by our sinful nature. Temptation was reinforced by no traitor within, by no welcoming bias of a depraved heart. To what extent his sense of its terrible power was diminished by this inward rectitude, we have no means of ascertaining.

Certain it is, however, that to him temptation

was both real and powerful. It appealed to those appetites and desires of human nature which are good and useful, when held in subjection to conscience and the love of God, but evil, when permitted to overrule the higher principles of that nature, and beget a spirit of disobedience to God, or impatience under suffering. A glance at Christ's great temptation, immediately after his baptism, will illustrate our meaning. It is on record, that he was led up by the Spirit into the wilderness; that during forty days he fasted, eating nothing, and that at the end of this period he was "a-hungered." Thus brief and simple is the narrative, saying little and yet saying much. For it may be inferred that the forty days were passed in a state of ecstatic devotion which raised him above the consciousness of physical wants. Then, however, the neglected body began to assert its claims once more, and terrible gnawings of hunger, such as are well-nigh intolerable, driving men to deeds of horror, were doubtless experienced by him. But there was no food to be obtained by natural means. Must, then, the awful sense of want be unappeased? Jesus knew himself to be the Son of God, possessed of miraculous power, and therefore able to relieve the pangs of hunger in a moment. Satan, too, was at hand and ready to whisper the word of temptation, — a word how skilfully chosen! "If thou be the Son of God, command that these stones be made bread." Here was a crafty insinuation that the voice from heaven at his baptism was unworthy of trust, and a challenge to prove its truthfulness by a miracle needed to assuage the pangs of hunger, — just such a miracle as a father would approve for the relief of his son. Is it possible to imagine a subtler temptation than this? To confound the adversary by an act of Messianic power, to gratify his own human reason by a visible proof of his divine sonship, and to remove his bodily suffering by the same act, — what could appear to human nature more desirable than this? What more seductive to a finite mind? The moral integrity of Christ, though perfect, would not surely prevent his realizing the force of such a temptation, however it might enable him, in absolute submission to the plan and will of God, promptly to repel it. We say "in absolute submission;" because it can hardly be supposed that the human understanding of Christ had as yet fully grasped the moral reasons for that plan, — a plan which excluded the use of miraculous power by the Saviour for his own relief or comfort. His lower nature, therefore, simply followed the intimations of the higher; to it the divine will was supreme, as it should be to us.

And these remarks furnish a brief reply to the

second part of the question proposed above, namely, Was the personal union of the human nature of Christ with the divine incompatible with its being tempted to evil? We answer, no; because the human knowledge of Christ was always partial, and partial knowledge opens the door to temptation. It will be recollected that, in our view, the complete personality of man comprises at least two elements, body and spirit, each distinct from the other in essence and attributes, yet brought mysteriously under the *vinculum* of a single consciousness, and so existing as a single self. It will also be recollected that, in the light of this analogy, the person of Christ was said to comprise at least three elements, a human body, a human spirit, and the eternal Word, each distinct from the others in essence and attributes, yet all united by a single consciousness. When, therefore, a certain condition of his body was represented in his consciousness by the sensation of thirst, he said, as a person, I thirst, and not, My body thirsts. So, too, when a certain condition of his human soul appeared in his consciousness, as ignorance, or sorrow, or desire, he predicated the same of himself as a person, and not of his human soul only. And likewise, when any act or fact of his divine nature, existing in his consciousness, was to be revealed, he affirmed this also of himself as a person, the God-man, and not simply of his Godhead. As the suffering due to certain conditions of his human body was felt by him in all its keenness; so the longing, or the anguish, due to certain conditions of his human soul, was felt by him in all its force. And since the faculties of Christ's human spirit had a truly normal though rapid growth in knowledge and power, they could have possessed during his earthly life but the smallest fraction of his divine knowledge, and must therefore have been subject to many of those forms of temptation which originate in imperfect knowledge.

It may therefore be said that Christ knew by actual experience the full power of temptation as addressed to human nature unperverted. And it may be supposed that the temptations which he met, regarded as allurements or provocations to sin, addressing his mind from without, were far greater than any to which other men have been exposed, — so much greater, indeed, as to counterbalance the advantage which he had in the moral integrity of his nature. This does not seem to us improbable. And if it was so in fact, then he knew by inward experience the power of temptation, as related to the actual state of man. Yet he did not sin; nay, more, it was morally impossible for him to sin. For the human side of his being was in high keeping, receiving light from the divine side, whenever this was required for his Messianic work, and evermore succored by the grace of the Holy Spirit, given to him without measure.

And this succor of the Spirit deserves particular consideration. For, to say nothing of the view, which has much in its favor, that the human nature of Christ was sanctified at conception by the personal agency of the Holy Ghost that came upon the Virgin, it seems most natural to suppose the symbolical descent of the Spirit upon Christ at his baptism, in the form of a dove, significant of an increased and miraculous working of that Spirit in the human soul of Christ during his earthly ministry. Nay, it has been thought by some, that all the miraculous action of the Holy Spirit, during this period, was confined to the person of Christ, or communicated to others, as it were, from his person, for temporary action. In support of this opinion, an appeal is made to the language of John (vii. 39), "But he spake this concerning the Spirit which those who believe on him should receive; for the Spirit was not yet;" that is, was not yet present with believers in his miraculous working, as he was to be on the day of Pentecost. But setting this aside, as not absolutely certain, we find in Acts i. 2 a distinct intimation of the Holy Spirit's action on the mind of Christ, while he was engaged in his Messianic work; for it speaks of "the day in which he was taken up, after that he, *through the Holy Ghost*, had given commandments unto the apostles whom he had chosen." Besides, it will be recollected that Luke speaks of him as "full of the Holy Ghost" after his baptism, and as being "led by the Spirit into the wilderness" (iv. 1). Now, if it is the work of the Spirit of God to prepare the faculties of the human soul to discern spiritual truth, to receive revelations from God, and to communicate them to men, it is reasonable to suppose that he may also have rendered a like service to the human soul of Christ, enabling it to receive all needed truth from his higher nature, the Word.

If, then, as we firmly believe, it is impossible to show that the moral integrity of Christ's human nature, or its personal union with the divine, as maintained by us, is incompatible with its being tempted to evil, the language of the New Testament, which affirms that he was thus tempted, does not require us to modify the view of his person set forth in our previous discussion. On the other hand, that view, which was drawn, we think, from the obvious meaning of the Scriptures, must be regarded as correct; and the Christian reader, whose mind has been disturbed by the startling theories of the day, may return with deep confidence to the doctrine of his fathers, old, indeed, but ever new and ever precious to the heart, that in Christ, Deity, acting as such, and Humanity, acting as such, were made one person; that Jesus, the Messiah, was the God-man, knowing the divine in a manner truly divine, and the human in a manner truly human, and filling perfectly the office of Mediator between God and men. It does not seem necessary to pursue the question further, and consider the particular temptations which were met and vanquished by Christ; for what has been said will be found applicable to them all; or if not, the subject involves so much of mystery as to suggest the admonition, "LET THY WORDS BE FEW."

PART SECOND.

THE WORK OF CHRIST;

OR, THE

ATONEMENT AS RELATED TO GOD AND MEN.

PART SECOND.

THE WORK OF CHRIST.

INTRODUCTION.

IF it cannot be said that the doctrine of the Atonement is now claiming the attention of as many writers as are discussing the doctrine of the Person of Christ, it can be said without hesitation that it still holds a central place in the hearts of Christians, and in the body of truth taught by the Word of God. A renewed examination of it, therefore, if made in a spirit of loyalty to Christ, must be welcome to those who love the Gospel for what it is, and not for the notice which is taken of it.

Besides, it can hardly be doubted that the doctrine of the Atonement, as it lies on the face of the Sacred Record and is related to the Person of Christ, is the chief though hidden spring of the attention which is given to the other doctrine named. The battle rages, and will never cease to rage, about the questions of Inspiration and the

Person of Christ; not, however, because they are questions which rise above the sphere of human science and have to do with the supernatural, thus enlisting curiosity and provoking doubt, but because the doctrine of atonement and reconciliation with God depends upon them. Dissolve their connection in human thought with this great spiritual interest of mankind, and they will soon lose their hold on the minds of the people. But so long as it is felt that the pardon of sin and the gift of eternal life may rest in the death of Christ, so long will the doctrines of his Person and of the Record which makes it known to us be matters of deep solicitude and inquiry.

The vital importance of our subject will therefore be conceded by all. And within a few years several writers have investigated it in works of considerable extent; some of them attempting to set this great doctrine in the moulds of human reason, that it may shine by its own light and commend itself fully to the mind of man, and others attempting to exhibit anew, in more convincing form, the scriptural evidence on which it rests, as held by them; but no one of these writers has so united spiritual insight and constructive imagination with reverence for the Word of God and a sound interpretation of its language, as to produce a work in all respects satisfactory. Most of them belong to the former class. Their aim has been to set forth a philosophy of the Atonement, or, in other words, to show that it rests on clear foundations of reason; but, in their anxiety to accomplish this perhaps desirable end, they have done violence, we fear, in some instances, to the obvious meaning of the Sacred Text. And if so, their fault is radical; for the Atonement is strictly a truth of revelation. Whether there is little or much analogous to it in the providential government of the world, as seen by us in the present life, we are made acquainted with the Atonement as a reality by the Word of God, and must receive it as described by that Word or reject it as unworthy of credence. No modification of the biblical doctrine, in however beautiful a theory it may result, is worthy of a moment's serious thought, for it must be without any solid basis.

But recent speculation has modified, as we believe, the biblical doctrine of the Atonement; and, for the most part, in one direction, by denying its relation to God and admitting only its relation to man, by affirming that it removes no obstacle in the divine mind to the forgiveness of sin in case of repentance, but simply operates on the sinner's heart and leads him to repent and believe. It does not reconcile God to the sinner, but only the sinner to God. Now this is a very imperfect view of the Atonement revealed by the Scriptures, and by its imperfection it forbids us to look upon the work of Christ as that in consideration of which our sins are forgiven. It bids us look upon his death as having simply a manward efficacy, as being nothing but an argument for repentance, a moral influence on the sinful soul; while the doctrine of justification by faith, as preached by the reformers, is rejected as an absurd error. Our first task must therefore be to show that the Atonement of Christ has a relation to the mind of God, and conditions the forgiveness of sin in case of repentance. Having established this fact, which is now frequently denied, it will be easy for us to show that the Atonement has also a relation to men, revealing to them the moral nature of God, and so, through the Spirit, drawing them to Christ.

Yet we do not give the first place to the effect which the Atonement has upon the mind and action of God, simply because this part of the biblical doctrine has been set aside by able writers, and is therefore more likely than any other to be called in question at the present time, but also because we hold it to be logically antecedent to the effect which the Atonement has upon the hearts of men, and indeed a principal cause of that effect. This might be made to appear, we believe, even though it were true that absolutely nothing but a revelation of the love of God can be used by the Holy Spirit in renewing and sanctifying the hearts of men. For no greater obstacle to the salvation of man can be imagined, than a feeling of the All Holy that sin ought not to be forgiven on the sole ground of repentance, that the suffering which is its just complement, or retribution, ought also in some real way to utter its voice; and no greater love can be imagined than a love which has removed that obstacle from the mind of God, by leading him to take suffering on himself, in the person of Christ. But it is not true that love is the only attribute of God which can be used by the Spirit in renewing and sanctifying the hearts of men. The righteousness of God may also be employed for the same purpose; for the law is our school-master unto Christ, and by it the justice of God is pre-eminently revealed. This will not be denied, unless it be by those who deny all distinction between righteousness and benevolence, justice and mercy, thus reducing the moral attributes of Jehovah to a single principle, that of love. But many take this course at the present time. It seems to them philosophical, and it accords with their desires. Some of them do not hesitate to say that love is the very essence of God, and the sum total of moral good in man. And it is very evident that this theory of the divine nature must have a powerful influence on the views of those who entertain it concerning the Atonement. It may therefore be well to look at it carefully, before turning to the passages of Scripture which treat of the latter doctrine.

Is it then true, that righteousness and benevolence are in principle one and the same? that justice and mercy are, when seen in the proper light, identical, or, at most, but different aspects of the same divine perfection? We find ourselves unable to accept this theory; and must beg the reader's attention to a few of the difficulties which overshadow it, and which have led us to reject it, hoping that he will not estimate their magnitude by the brevity of our discussion.

1. The theory in question is inconsistent with the common language and judgment of mankind. Everywhere men speak of uprightness and benevolence as distinct qualities of character. There is probably no language which fails to express these qualities by separate terms, no people which regards justice as one with grace. The two must therefore be distinguishable, not by some subtle peculiarity which only the cultivated mind is able to detect, but by broad and obvious features which the plain sense of the people recognizes. If, now, it be said that the language and judgment of the multitude are often superficial, noting the apparent difference while overlooking the real and deeper unity, we freely admit that this is sometimes true.

But not always nor generally. That which commends itself to the common intelligence of the race, to the good sense of the great mass of mankind, is not likely to be altogether a mistake. There is at least a presumption in its favor, which only clear and strong evidence can overcome; and this presumption, in the present case, lies directly in the way of identifying the qualities of righteousness and benevolence, or of resolving all the moral perfections of God into the one principle of love.

2. The theory in question is inconsistent with the customary language of Scripture. This statement will not be gainsaid by any careful reader of the Word. Thus, the apostle remarks that "Scarcely for a righteous man will one die, yet peradventure for a good man some would even dare to die," — making a clear distinction between righteousness and goodness, or justice and love. And this distinction pervades the language of the Sacred Record from first to last. It is applied in almost numberless places to the attributes of God; and not unfrequently to those of man. But it may be urged that the Bible, appealing to the common sense of the many and not to the finer discrimination of the few, must needs accommodate itself to popular opinion, whenever it can do so without sacrificing essential truth, and may there-

fore adopt distinctions which are in fact unreal. And if this be so, our second objection, it is said, is simply identical with the first. But we do not accept the representation just made as correct. However popular the style of Scripture may be, no language can be truer than its language to the facts of our moral and religious consciousness. If then we distrust its account of the divine character, we are left in total darkness. Besides, those who teach that righteousness and love are really the same, do not look upon this as a non-essential truth. It shapes their whole theory of law and penalty. It determines their view of the Atonement. It modifies their explanation of the scriptural terms, pardon and justification. It is the seed-truth of their religious thought. We cannot therefore concede to them the privilege of calling this a non-essential truth which the Word of God, by accommodating itself to the judgment of mankind, has failed to reveal.

But a more plausible answer to our objection is made by saying, that Christ himself refers the entire moral law to one command, that of love. This is indeed true; and it is true because the great obstacle to perfect virtue in men is a want of that love which the law requires; it is true, not because that love comprises, but because it conditions all other right action. Let selfishness be displaced by that love, and human nature would be at once restored to its normal state; the voice of conscience would always be obeyed. Hence the Word of God, addressing itself to the actual condition of men, enforces that claim of the eternal law of right which disregarded leads to the disregard of every other, and which obeyed ensures the obedience of all the rest. In this sense all the law and the prophets hang on the first and great commandment. But the language of Christ does not authorize us to go farther than this, and reduce all virtue in man and holiness in God to a single affection.

3. The theory in question is incompatible with the clearest decisions of our moral judgment. For upon close consideration we perceive that benevolence is right, but not that right is benevolence. Right is more comprehensive than love, and we can imagine circumstances in which the dictates of the former would not coincide with those of the latter.

We have called attention to this point, because of the relation which it has to the doctrine of the Atonement. And if the reader who had received without careful examination the popular theory in question finds his confidence in it so far shaken that he will go to the Scriptures with a mind open to instruction, it is enough. Our knowledge in respect to the nature and ends of the Atonement must be drawn exclusively from the sacred oracles; and by a reverent study of their words we may hope to ascertain the essential facts and principles comprised in that wondrous work of God.

NOTE.—For a further discussion of certain questions considered in the foregoing, see Chapter I. in the "Examination of the Vicarious Sacrifice of Dr. Bushnell," in Part III.

CHAPTER I.

THE ATONEMENT AS RELATED TO GOD.

I. A GROUND FOR RENEWING AND PARDONING GRACE.

AS it is our purpose to advance step by step to a position where the power and nature of the Atonement may be clearly seen, it will be enough to define it, with reference to our immediate object, as *that in consideration of which God renews the hearts and pardons the sins of all who are saved.* In other words, it has furnished him with a good and sufficient reason for leading men by special grace to repentance, and for remitting their sins in case of repentance. In still other, and perhaps more exact terms, it has removed an obstacle, in the mind of God, to the exercise of his regenerating and forgiving grace. If these statements, or either of them, be correct, then surely the Atonement has relations to God no less essential than its relations to men; it is a condition of his grace to them, as well as a moral power to draw them to him.

And in support of this position, we refer to the apostolic declaration: "Him hath God exalted a Prince and a Saviour, to give repentance unto Israel and remission of sins."[1] Plainly the work of Christ after his ascension is here described; and this language may be compared with the words of Peter on the day of Pentecost: "Therefore, having been exalted to the right hand of God, and having received the promise of the Holy Spirit from the Father, he hath poured out this, which ye now see and hear."[2] From the similarity of these passages it is probable, if not certain, that giving "repentance" and "pouring out the Spirit" were closely connected in the apostle's mind, the latter specifying the crowning agency employed by the Saviour, and the former stating the chief result of that agency. No explicit reference is made in either of them to the moral power of Christ's earthly life, as producing repentance, or to the story of his cross, as subduing rebellion in the selfish will. Admitting, then, as we thankfully do, the great moral influence of the Atonement on the hearts of men, we do not find that influence expressed by the words, "to give repentance unto Israel,"—much less in the farther clause, "and remission of sins;" but the Saviour is set before us by this language in his regal state, exercising

[1] Acts v. 31. [2] Acts ii. 33.

the prerogatives of a divine Ruler, giving and forgiving as Mediatorial King. And his Headship over all is, as Paul teaches, a reward for his suffering, even unto death, in behalf of men. "Wherefore," — that is, on account of this humiliation and suffering,—"God also hath highly exalted him, and given him a name which is above every name." Through him, then, or in consideration of his work, God saves the elect, by renewing their hearts, forgiving their sins, and keeping them by divine power through faith unto eternal life. "Neither is there salvation in any other; for there is no other name under heaven, given among men, whereby we must be saved."[1] "Through this man is preached the forgiveness of sins, and by him all that believe are justified."[2] Now, it is evident that pardon and justification are represented in this passage as being, in the order of nature, subsequent to faith; and therefore, if it could be fairly supposed, as it cannot, that the latter is here traced by the apostle to the moral influence of Christ, it would still be true that the former are said to be given by him, or through him, and in no other way, — a fact which can only be explained by admitting that his Atonement removed an obstacle existing in the mind of God to their pardon. To say that forgiveness of sins is granted by or through him ex-

[1] Acts iv. 12. [2] Acts xiii. 38, 39.

clusively, is, in view of all the circumstances, equivalent to saying that it is granted in consideration of his atoning death. This will be made certain before we finish our discussion of the topic.

An argument for our view, or definition, may also be drawn from those passages of Scripture which represent Christ as interceding with God for his people. Thus Paul speaks of "Christ that died, yea, rather, that is risen again, who is even at the right hand of God, who also maketh intercession for us."[1] John affirms that "if any one sin, we have an Advocate with the Father, Jesus Christ the righteous."[2] And the Epistle to the Hebrews declares that "he is able to save them to the uttermost who come unto God by him, seeing he ever liveth to make intercession for them,"[3] as also, in another place, that "Christ is entered into heaven itself, now to appear in the presence of God for us."[4] It is evident, from these passages, that the sacred writers looked upon the presence of Christ in heaven as a constant plea for the favor of God to believers, as an all-sufficient reason for the bestowal of grace upon the followers of Jesus. And it is equally evident, from the connection in which every one of these expressions is found, that their writers saw in Christ such a plea, or reason, because he had offered himself a sacrifice for the sins

[1] Ro. viii. 34. [2] 1 John ii. 1. [3] Heb. vii. 25. [4] Ib. ix. 24.

of the people. To say, then, that this language, which speaks of Christ's appearing in the presence of God and making intercession for us, really means that, read in the light of his exalted state, the story of his earthly mission is rendered more effective and salutary in its influence on man, is to pervert the plain testimony of Scripture, and deny that to be a motive to the mind of God which his Word affirms to be such a motive. Great as is the love of God to men, he looks not upon them alone, but upon Jesus Christ, who suffered, the just for the unjust; and in response to the plea which the Redeemer's presence makes, bestows grace and salvation upon the guilty. All this, at least, must be involved in the declaration that Christ intercedes in our behalf with the Father; and it confirms our position that renewing and pardoning grace are given in consideration of the Atonement.

And, lastly, the Apostle Paul declares that by the death of Christ the world was put in such a relation to God, that he could treat it with favor, instead of wrath. For, after saying that Christ died for the ungodly, for sinners, he proceeds thus, "Much more then, having now been justified in his blood, we shall be saved from wrath through him. For if, when we were sinners, we were reconciled to God by the death of his Son, much more, having been reconciled, we shall be saved in his life."[1] We beg the reader's close attention to this passage; for while it seems, at first sight, to speak of the spiritual attitude of men towards God, and not of God towards men, the course of thought which the apostle gives in this connection favors another view. The second of these verses manifestly reproduces and confirms the argument of the first; but the first speaks of justification, not as being found in repentance, but rather in the blood of Christ, and of salvation from the wrath to come as the sure result of justification in that blood. For salvation, according to the apostle, is not rooted primarily in human action, but in divine grace. Then he confirms this statement by another, in the same line of thought: "For if, when we were the objects of God's wrath, like rebels whom their king counts as enemies, we were put in a condition to receive his favor, by the death of his Son, much more, having been put in that condition, shall we be saved in his life." A similar use of the word "enemies" may be seen in a later section of this letter,[2] where Paul speaks to the Gentiles respecting the Jews as being, "with regard to the gospel, enemies for your sakes, but with regard to the election, beloved for the fathers' sakes." In this place the antithetic term, "beloved," fixes the interpretation of the word "enemies;" it must signify objects of

[1] Rom. v. 9, 10. [2] Rom. xi. 28.

displeasure. Moreover, the Greek words which are translated, "We were reconciled to God," may signify either the turning away of God's wrath from us, or of our hatred from him. They have the former meaning in the passage before us; the reconciliation referred to having been effected by the death of Christ, which, by the new relation in which it placed men, removed from the divine mind an obstacle to the bestowal of his grace upon them. This explanation is confirmed by the last clause of the next verse, which should be thus translated: "Through whom we have now received the reconciliation," namely, the reconciliation which was effected on God's part by the death of Christ, and which is accepted on our part by an act of simple faith.

To the passage now examined may be added another from the second letter of Paul to the Corinthians. It represents the message given to the apostles for men thus: "How that God in Christ reconciled the world to himself, not imputing to them their transgressions."[1]—"Observe," says Alford, "that the reconciliation spoken of in this verse is that of *God to us* absolutely and objectively, through his Son; that whereby he can complacently behold and endure a sinful world, and receive all who come to him by Christ." In the next verse the Corinthians are exhorted to a

[1] 2 Cor. v. 19, 20.

subjective and responsive reconciliation: "We pray you in Christ's stead, be ye reconciled to God." By the death of his Son, God has removed every obstacle on his part to harmony between himself and mankind, and now calls upon them to accept his proffered grace. To him the one great and well-nigh insuperable obstacle to concord was one rising up from the depths of his own holy nature, and that has been put out of the way, so that his good-will flows out freely towards men. He has thus established harmony between himself and the world. If there be any more separation, it must be due to their rejecting peace and choosing wrath.

For these reasons, to go no farther, we believe that the Atonement is revealed to us by the Word of God as that in consideration of which renewing and forgiving grace is bestowed on all who are saved. With this fact established, we may take another step, and examine yet more closely the Atonement in its relation to God.

II. AN ILLUSTRATION OF GOD'S RIGHTEOUSNESS.

It has been shown by us already that righteousness and love are not one and the same in a moral being; and it may now be added, that both of them are principles of action, and both sacred. In a Being, therefore, who is absolutely perfect, both of them will be sure to find expression, and perhaps we may say an equally clear expression. The claims of righteousness will not be sacrificed to those of benevolence, nor the claims of benevolence to those of righteousness. The wisdom of such a Being will provide a channel through which these kindred perfections of his nature may flow out in action.

But if, in dealing with sinners for their salvation, no account is taken of the just penalty of sin, but only of its hurtful power, the claims of righteousness seem to be disregarded. For the penalty of sin is prescribed by righteousness as that which answers to the nature of sin, and therefore ought to be inflicted; no moral axiom being more certain than this, that everything should be treated according to its real nature. Wrong must be recognized and met as wrong, misfortune as misfortune; guilt must be treated as guilt, and innocence as innocence. And, apart from the Atonement, the only way in which the ill-desert of sin is recognized and met by the Supreme Ruler, is by putting upon the sinner the loss and suffering which are its condign punishment. Hence, as the ill-desert of sin in those who are saved through the Atonement is not met by a just penalty inflicted on them, it must be met in some other way; and we understand the Scriptures to teach that it has been met by the Atonement, which took up into itself and expressed, with equal clearness, both the righteousness and the love of God. But as all who recognize the authority of Scripture admit that the death of Christ was a signal illustration of the divine love, we shall fix our attention for the present on those passages which prove that it was also an illustration of the divine righteousness.

Of these passages the most important and remarkable is the following, which we ask the privilege of translating from the Greek; "Being justified freely by his grace, through the redemption that is in Christ Jesus; whom God set forth as a propitiation, through faith, in his blood, for the exhibition of his righteousness, because of the passing by of the sins before committed in the forbearance of God; for the exhibition of his righteousness in the present time, that he may be just and the justifier of him who believeth in Jesus."[1]

[1] Rom. iii. 24, 26. This text is so important that I will add the translation of the Am. Bible Union, of Dean Alford, and of Dr. Noyes. They will be seen to agree substantially with my own. The B. U. revision reads thus: "Being justified freely by his grace, through the redemption that is in Christ Jesus; whom God set forth as a propitiation through faith by his blood, for the exhibition of his righteousness, because of the passing over of the sins before committed in the forbearance of God; for the exhibition of his righteousness in the present time, that he may be just, and the justifier of him who believes in Jesus." Alford translates as follows: "Being justified freely by his grace, through the redemption that is in Christ Jesus; whom God set forth as a propitiation through faith by his blood, for the showing forth of his righteous-

This passage seems to have been written for the very purpose of rendering forever vain and futile any attempt to limit the efficacy of the Atonement to its moral influence over men. For the apostle distinctly specifies the exhibition of God's righteousness as a proximate end of Christ's death. And he declares that this exhibition was called for by the circumstance that, in his treatment of sinners both before and since the time of Christ, God had ignored, to a certain extent, the claims of righteousness, passing by in his forbearance the sins committed in the former period, without inflicting upon their authors condign punishment, and accepting as righteous, in the latter period, all men, however sinful, who believe in Jesus. Hence this course of action must be complemented by the Atonement, in order that the righteousness of God may be suitably revealed to men, or may even remain untarnished in himself; in order that he may be, and may be known to be, a just moral Governor of the race. In other words, the Atone-

ness, because of the passing over of the former sins, in the forbearance of God; for the showing forth of his righteousness in this present time, that he may be just, and the justifier of him who is of faith in Jesus." And Noyes, a Unitarian, gives the following version: "Being accepted as righteous freely, by his grace, through the redemption that is in Christ Jesus, whom in his blood through faith God hath set forth as a propitiatory sacrifice, in order to manifest his righteousness, on account of his passing by, in his forbearance, the sins committed in former times; in order to manifest his righteousness at the present time, so that he may be righteous, and accept as righteous him who hath faith."

ment, as an exercise and exhibition of God's judicial righteousness, is presupposed by his treatment of sinners from the first. Without it, he could not have passed by the sins of former times, or forgiven those of later times. Long before it was made, he anticipated it and adjusted his action to it, and to the end of time it will be a sufficient reason for the exercise of his saving grace.

If the language of Paul does not mean this, and precisely this, it must be impossible to ascertain what any language does mean; for every word and clause, from first to last, seems to be directed, like the strokes of a sculptor's chisel, only with a higher intelligence, to the production of this particular and well-defined thought. In making this statement we have in mind the original text, and not the common version of that text; for, as will be seen by our translation given above, we do not regard the common version, in this particular instance, as altogether exact. Especially has it failed in reproducing the clause which we have rendered, "because of the passing by of the sins before committed in the forbearance of God." The original of this clause is eminently exact, word answering to word with perfect consistency, and it cannot mean what is suggested by the common version, "for the remission of sins that are past through the forbearance of God." For if the apostle had spoken of the remission of sins, he would have connected it with the grace, and not with the forbearance of God. Grace remits the penalty and receives into favor; forbearance endures the sin without executing the penalty. The Greek word translated forbearance is associated in no other passage, either instrumentally or causally, with the forgiveness of sins. Besides, the word translated "remission" occurs nowhere else in the New Testament, and properly signifies "passing by." This fact alone is decisive in favor of our rendering. And as no definite provision was revealed to the ancient Israelites for the pardon of great moral offences through an adequate sacrifice, God's treatment of those who were guilty of such offences — and all, even the most devout, were thus guilty — must have seemed to them a sort of passing by of their sins, rather than a full and assured remission of them. Hence the language of the Epistle to the Hebrews in two most interesting passages: "For if the blood of bulls, and of goats, and the ashes of a heifer, sprinkling the unclean, sanctifieth to the purifying of the flesh; how much more shall the blood of Christ, who through the eternal Spirit offered himself without spot unto God, purge your conscience from dead works to serve the living God? And for this cause he is the Mediator of the New Testament, that by means of death, for the redemption of the transgressions under the first Testament, they which are called might receive the promise of the eternal inheritance."[1]

III. A PROPITIATION FOR SINS.

Having shown that the Atonement is that in consideration of which God bestows his renewing and pardoning grace on those who are saved, and that it has this relation to saving grace because it was an exhibition of God's righteousness, we are prepared to take another step, and show from the Scriptures how it took up into itself and expressed that righteousness. For it cannot be denied that the Atonement, if it was an exhibition of God's righteousness, must also have been in some way an exercise of it. It must at least be traceable without difficulty to his love of moral rectitude, and his opposition to sin. For an act which can be referred to mere power or wisdom or benevolence as its source, manifests power, wisdom, or benevolence, but not distinctively righteousness. Says Dr. Hodge: "The Atonement is an exhibition of God's purpose to maintain his law and inflict its penalty — *because it involves the execution of that penalty*. It is this which gives it all its power. It would be no exhibition of justice, if it were not an exercise of justice; it would not teach that the

[1] Heb. ix. 14, 15 (cf. xi. 40.)

penalty of the law must be inflicted, unless it was inflicted." Now, without adopting this expression of Dr. Hodge as an exact equivalent of our own, without saying as yet that righteousness and justice are synonymous in speaking of the Atonement, we do say that righteousness cannot be exhibited except as it is exercised, and hence that the Atonement took up into itself and expressed the righteousness of God. How it did this we must now attempt to show. And, for this purpose, we do not need a clearer statement, at the outset, than is furnished by the great passage which has been already quoted: "Being justified freely by his grace, through the redemption that is in Christ Jesus; whom God set forth as a propitiation, through faith, in his blood, for the exhibition of his righteousness, because of the passing by of the sins before committed, in the forbearance of God; for the exhibition of his righteousness in the present time, that he may be just and the justifier of him who believeth in Jesus." Here we are told that *the righteousness of God was exhibited by setting forth Christ in his blood as a propitiatory sacrifice.* And two questions are naturally suggested by this statement: namely, Who, in the first instance, was made propitious by this sacrifice? And how and why did the blood of Christ have this peculiar effect? Let us attempt a reply to these important questions.

The word which we have rendered "propitiation" is strictly an adjective, signifying "propitiatory;" and what the apostle affirms is this: that Christ was set forth in his blood as *propitiatory*, that is, as making one or each of the parties at variance merciful or propitious to the other. Was it the ruler who was to be made favorable to the rebel, or the rebel to the ruler? — the offended sovereign to the offending subject, or the offending subject to the offended sovereign? If we look at the use of the verb from which the adjective in question is derived, it will be natural to conclude that, in the case before us, God was the party propitiated; for in classic writers, Josephus included, this verb signifies to appease or make propitious, whether by sacrifice, or gift, or song; and the object of it is — in Homer always, and in others almost always — a god. Yet Herodotus speaks of propiating men whom one has injured, by paying them divine honors after death. But the point to be noted is this, that the object of the verb is always the party which is conceived of as having been wronged or offended. Men are never propitiated by gods.

The same verb occurs in two passages of the New Testament. In one of these — the prayer of the publican — it has the passive form and sense: "God, be merciful to me a sinner."[1] Now, the publican did not pray that his own heart might be changed and made friendly to God, but rather that God would be gracious to him, though a sinner. And his prayer was answered. Was it an error, mistaking the end to be secured? — assuming that God must be reconciled to the sinner, and not merely the sinner to God? No one will assert this; for Christ himself sanctioned the prayer, if he did not originate it. Besides, there is some reason to suppose that the most important word put into the publican's prayer by the Saviour was meant to include a reference to atonement by sacrifice; for neither the circumstance marked by the words, "Two men went up *into the temple* to pray," nor the peculiar language of Jesus concerning the result of their praying, "I say unto you, this man went down to his house *justified* rather than the other," should be overlooked in studying the passage. And, bearing in mind these clauses, we may thus paraphrase the publican's cry: "O God, be thou propitiated, by the sacrifices of thine house, to me, a sinner." He did not, like the Pharisee, ask God to be merciful to him on account of his good works, or even on account

[1] Luke xviii. 13.

of his repentance, but rather in consideration of the propitiatory sacrifice which was making its appeal from the altar. This seems to be a natural view of the publican's comprehensive petition.

In the only other passage where the same verb occurs (Heb. ii. 18), it has, though in the middle voice, an active sense, and is translated, "to make reconciliation," namely, "for the sins of the people." This may be explained, with Winer, as an elliptical expression, meaning, "to propitiate God for the sins of the people,"—an interpretation which agrees with the classical use of the word; or it may be explained by the Hebrew phrase, signifying "to make atonement for sins,"—which, again, is simply the expression, "to cover over sins," figuratively used. Hence the sacred writers apply the word in question "to one who performs an act, the object of which is *sin*, and the effect of which is that sin shall cease to awaken God's wrath towards men. Expiation interposes between wrath and sin, so that the latter is covered over." (Moll.)

It may then be safely inferred from the use of this verb, both in classical writers and in the New Testament, that it does not denote the effect of such an act as sacrifice upon men in changing their spiritual attitude towards God, but rather the effect of such an act in covering sin, or bringing the sinner into relations where God can properly show favor to him, perhaps I might say, in changing the governmental attitude of God towards sinners. And the same result would follow an examination of the adjective derived from this verb. Hence we say that the proximate effect of propitiation is to secure the exercise of God's grace towards the guilty; which effect is secured, not by working a change in their moral disposition, — for then atonement and regeneration would be the same, — but by putting them in a new relation to law and justice. In consequence of this, the wrath of God towards sinners gives place to mercy. And the conclusion now reached may be fortified by an appeal to the Mosaic law concerning sacrifices for sin, and especially concerning the sin offering.

It appears, from Lev. xvii. 10, 11, that Jehovah strictly forbade his people to eat any manner of blood, assigning the reason for this prohibition in the following words: "For the life of the flesh is in the blood, and I have given it to you upon the altar to atone for your souls (or lives); for the blood atones by the life." This passage makes it certain that atonement by sacrifice was ordained of God for his people, and was completed by covering, in a figure, the object laden with sin; for the word translated "to atone," literally signifies "to cover." The same passage teaches, also, that the blood of an animal slain for the purpose was chosen for this emblematical cover, because blood is the seat of life, and therefore, when shed, a natural sign and symbol of death. By making this last remark, we part company with those who restrict the efficacy of the Atonement to its moral influence over men; for they insist that the blood offered in sacrifice was in no sense a symbol of death; it represented life, and nothing but life, for death is polluting. To this we reply as follows: —

1. The Scriptures nowhere speak of death as unclean or polluting.

2. The law provides that other parts of the animal offered in sacrifice should come upon the altar. Were they impure because bereft of life? If the absence of life makes the blood unclean, it must surely make every other part of the animal unclean; if it does not make the other parts impure, neither can it make the blood impure.

3. The slaying of the animal offered in sacrifice is often and formally prescribed; so often, indeed, as to prove beyond a reasonable doubt that it was an important part of the sacrificial rite.

4. Bread and wine in the Lord's Supper represent the body and blood of Christ, — the body broken and the blood poured out, in sacrifice for us. But the apostle writes to the Corinthians:

"As often as ye eat this bread, and drink this cup, ye do show the Lord's *death*, till he come."

We have directed attention to this point,[1] because the truth here is essential to a correct view of the sin-offering among the Jews, and, through that, explanatory of the great sacrifice upon Calvary; and also because the same truth is a fatal objection to the theory of those who ascribe only a manward and moral efficacy to the Atonement. For if the death of the animal offered in sacrifice for sin was indispensable to the meaning and effect of the sacrifice, the old doctrine that, this animal taking the sinner's place, its death took the place of the sinner's death, at once emerges into clearest light, and will not be remanded into darkness. Moreover, the death which *takes the place of a penal death*, so as to meet the claims of righteousness, may naturally be looked upon as in some sense the penalty due to the sinner and borne by his substitute. And this is the honored doctrine of a vicarious Atonement, a doctrine which has given peace to many a troubled conscience and courage to many a sinking heart, a doctrine which turns the eye away from self and the effect of truth upon self, and fixes it upon Christ and his righteousness, being, therefore, as some who

[1] For a further discussion of this topic, see Part Third, Ch. II., 5.

reject it acknowledge, the best form of thought to work true freedom and grace in the heart.

The view which has now been given of the sin-offering may be confirmed by several considerations. This offering was always brought for sin, and generally for a particular sin. It was also named "sin," because of its exclusive relation to the same. Before slaying his prescribed victim, the offerer laid his hands on its head, for the purpose of transferring to it, by the language of symbol, his own guilt. Again, more prominence was given in this kind of sacrifice than in any other to the sprinkling of the blood, doubtless because the idea of death, the penalty of sin, was to be emphasized. Besides, the effect of this sprinkling was to atone for the offerer or his sin, that is, to cover him or it ideally with the victim's blood. And, finally, the end secured by this atonement was the forgiveness of the offerer's sin. (See Lev. iv. v.) So obviously do these facts sustain our view of the sin-offering, that it seems unnecessary to do more than specify them. Indeed, it would require some ingenuity, in "making the worse appear the better reason," to turn away the reader's mind from their evident bearing.

There is, however, another and more general fact which merits attention at this point, namely, that, "apart from the ceremonial prescribed for a particular day once a year, the Jewish sacrifices did not profess to atone for violations of the moral law. Only involuntary ceremonial offences, which were but the symbols of real moral transgressions," together with civil offences, which affected one's standing as a member of an earthly and typical kingdom, "could be expiated by sacrifices which were but the symbols of the real Atonement for sin." And it is at least doubtful, whether the sacrifices for sins which were offered on the great day of Atonement had respect to violations of the moral law. The language, to be sure, is unqualified: "All the iniquities of the children of Israel and all their transgressions in all their sins;" but these expressions ought perhaps to be interpreted by the other provisions of the law, and, if so, restricted to the iniquities, transgressions, and sins for which, in other instances, atonement could be made by animal sacrifice. There was no provision for pardon, through sacrifice, of outbreaking violations of the moral law, such as idolatry, blasphemy, murder, cursing of parents, man-stealing, or for heart-sins, such as anger, malice, hatred, pride, avarice, want of love to God and man. Hence the language of David after the murder of Uriah: "Thou desirest not sacrifice, else would I give it; thou delightest not in burnt offering;" and the same view may be taken of certain passages of the prophetic books which represent sacrifices as worthless. For they only availed to secure pardon for minor infractions of the civil or ceremonial law of the Jews. They only "sanctified to the purifying of the flesh." And therefore when men, like David, guilty of sins for which the law failed to prescribe any atonement, were not cut off by the judgment of heaven, God must have seemed to pass by in his forbearance their great offences, even as Paul declares in the passage quoted near the beginning of our article.

Yet "without shedding of blood there is no remission;" and the grace which was shown to good men of old anticipated and rested upon the sacrifice of Christ. The sin-offering of the Jewish economy illustrated, within the sphere of temporal relations and an earthly kingdom, the principles of the divine government within the sphere of eternal relations and a spiritual kingdom. As the Jewish nation was but a figure of the true spiritual Israel, so the Jewish sacrifices were but figures of the one Perfect Sacrifice; and as, by the former, transgressors of the civil or ceremonial law obtained forgiveness and all the privileges of the earthly kingdom, so, by the latter, transgressors of the eternal law obtain forgiveness and citizenship in heaven. By the Mosaic economy principles were taught, hopes inspired, and moulds of language prepared, which belong to a higher economy; but the shadow could not give the substance; spiritual life and peace were then, as now, dependent on the work of Christ; "the law could never, with those sacrifices which they offered year by year continually, make the comers thereunto perfect," but it could and did, by those sacrifices, and especially by the sin-offering, foreshadow the sacrifice on Calvary, where Christ suffered, the just for the unjust, to bring us to God. And the fact that, in the sin-offering, the death of the animal took the place of the death due to the offerer for his sin, and so met and ratified the claims of righteousness, proves that the same was true on a higher plane of the death of Christ; as sacrificial, propitiatory, it took upon itself and met the claims of eternal righteousness for sinners.

Professor Smeaton uses the following language in respect to the Jewish sacrifices: "What did the sacrifices effect? They sanctified to the purifying of the flesh, — that is, cleansed the worshipper ceremonially; for it is better to say ceremonially than corporeally, as the latter word scarcely defines the result. They could effect nothing more, nor was more intended. They did not, and could not, make the worshipper perfect as pertaining to the conscience (Heb. ix. 9); they could not remove the conscience of sin, or the conscious knowledge of sin (x. 2); they could not put away sin as to the objective guilt (x. 4). The Jewish sacrifices could do none of these things, and never were intended to come into that inner circle where man, as a moral and responsible creature under a holy, spiritual law, has to do as a guilty sinner with a righteous and holy God. But they were meant to do something in their true sphere; they put away ceremonial defilement, temporal punishment, and that exclusion from the sanctuary and the fellowship of God's people to which ceremonial defilement exposed. . . But they did more; they also taught important things. They taught (1,) that sacrifices were of grace on the part of God; (2,) that they were vicarious; (3,) that they were a satisfaction for the sins of the people," that is, for certain "involuntary states of body, or some inevitable violation of those positive laws by which Israel was separated by God from other nations" (pp. 384, 385). It may be well to give also in this place the view of Dr. Ferdinand Weber, in his work *On the Wrath of God*, "Vom Zorne Gottes," concerning the effect of the Jewish sacrifices. He attempts to show, from the Word of God, that since the fall the history of mankind may be regarded as illustrating either the divine wrath or love. "The period of the Old Testament was one of *forbearance*, ἀνοχή, or sparing patience; wrath was as yet unappeased, but love, which had formed the purpose of expiation, adopted a provisional means of expiation and salvation, so that it was possible for man to cover himself from wrath and take his stand in love; and prophecy revealed a day of Jehovah in prospect, when sin would be finally expiated, while all those who should despise recovering love would be finally judged, — thus a day for the revelation of both love and wrath. This day of Jehovah began with the work of Jesus Christ, who, by the offering of himself, made a true expiation." He appeals to several passages of the New Testament in proof of the statement, that for the sins committed before the sacrifice of Christ there was no full or proper forgiveness, but only a passing by or overlooking, *paresis;* that because those sins were only passed by, Christ's sacrifice was necessary in order to make atonement for them, and that the period which began with the sacrifice of Christ was a new one, ὁ νῦν καιρός. To give his view in his own words, we say: —

"1. *That* man is in need of an atonement is proved beyond a doubt by the *sacrifices* instituted by God himself. For these bear witness that God is angry on account of sin, and will not endure the sinner without a covering before his face. But they also bear witness that Jehovah will give to man the pardon of sin, or will let himself be reconciled with man. As the law testifies aloud with its curse of the wrath of God, so the sacrifices proclaim aloud the propitiation of the divine wrath, (Lev. xvii. 11.) But the way which the sacrifices show for the propitiation of the divine wrath is that of *vicarious satisfaction*. There could have been nothing said of forgiveness, of grace and reconciliation, but only of punishment of sin or fulfilling divine wrath, had not a *vicarious* satisfaction been offered in the propitiatory sacrifice by another than man. . . .

"2. The Jewish sacrifices offered the life of an animal; but this was no true equivalent, it was rather but the image of an equivalent. Hence its effect was only that of sparing or overlooking; and therefore faith, which felt the limit and longed after a full removal of wrath, sought for a better equivalent. Finding then the *true* sacrifice in a broken heart, it confesses that sin has forfeited life, and that the true equivalent for sin committed would be the life of the sinner himself. But this he cannot bring for himself, nor can another bring it (Ps. xlix. 9) ; hence he must trust the Lord, who is merciful, to redeem in *his own* way Israel from all his sins.

"3. Israel, indeed, had already before its eyes the vicarious satisfaction of a Mediator between Jehovah and Israel, in the person of Moses, who offered his life for Israel's guilt. Moreover, the sufferings of David and the prophets, as their calling implied, were a faint reflection of the sufferings of a Mediator, who should make expiation for his people; but in all this and much besides there were only slight hints for the solution of the question, and not that solution itself. The Mosaic sacrifices, as the whole law, were a mystery which needed a divine explanation by a special revelation. And this was given by prophecy which spoke of the day of the Lord as a day of judgment and of reconciliation." (S. 179,180.)

It will be seen at once that this view of Weber does not differ essentially from the one maintained by us. In his judgment, as well as in ours, the only sacrifice which avails for the remission of sins against the moral law is that of Christ; but he supposes that the Jewish sacrifices prevented immediate punishment, hid away sin, as it were, from the eye of Jehovah, until Christ's death met the claims of a violated law, and the sinner was assured of pardon; while we suppose that the Jewish sacrificial worship was pre-eminently symbolical and typical, securing the pardon of civil and ritual offences, and so foreshadowing the great sacrifice which would avail in the higher realm of strictly moral government and spiritual action.

IV. CHRIST'S SUFFERINGS PENAL.

The result of our discussion thus far may be summed up in the following statements: That the Atonement is related to God, inasmuch as it removed from his mind an obstacle to the bestowal of renewing and forgiving grace upon sinners; that it effected this removal by meeting in some way the claims of divine righteousness, and thereby exhibiting that righteousness; and that it met those claims, in great part at least, by the voluntary death of Christ, which death he suffered as the penalty due to men for their sins. It will be seen that these different statements are strictly harmonious; that the first is explained by the second, and the second by the third, and indeed that they are so bound together by the Scriptures as to form a threefold cord not easily broken. But the last statement, especially, has met with so much opposition from good men that it calls for yet further consideration. We propose, therefore, to devote a little space to a confirmation of it; yet without looking beyond the Scriptures for evidence; for if the authority of the Bible is admitted by our readers, that evidence will be conclusive, while, if it is not, the doctrine of the Atonement will be likely to share the same fate in their minds with every other doctrine peculiar to Christianity. For ourselves the authority of the Bible is supreme, and the Bible teaches, we believe, that Christ suffered death as the penalty due to men for their sins. What that death was, how much pain of body and anguish of soul it involved, and what was the spiritual process by which this anguish was experienced, may be reserved for another occasion. Our present task is to justify the third statement given above by additional evidence from the Word of God.

And, first, by simply putting together the two facts, that death is the penalty of sin and that Christ must needs die in order to save sinners, we are led at once to the statement in question, and, especially, when we bear in mind the emphasis with which the necessity of Christ's death is taught by the Scriptures. For the Saviour said to his disciples, "The Son of man must suffer many things . . . and be put to death;" "The Son of man must be delivered into the hands of men;" "That which is written must be fulfilled in me, . . and he was reckoned with transgressors;"[1] and the Epistle to the Hebrews declares that "every high-priest is ordained to offer gifts and sacrifices;" from which, as Christ was a high-priest, the conclusion naturally follows: "Wherefore it is of necessity that this man have somewhat also to offer." And this

[1] Mark viii. 31; Luke ix. 44; xxii. 37.

necessary offering the epistle goes on to describe as "his own blood," or "himself offered without spot unto God."[1] In perfect agreement with these sentences is the whole tenor of apostolic teaching, and, especially, the meaning of the two ordinances which the Saviour delivered to his disciples. They both commemorate his death, — not his incarnation, nor his holy life, nor his agony in the garden, — but his death, as the central and controlling fact of his mediatorial work. For this he came into the world, "not to be ministered unto, but to minister, and give his life a ransom for many." For this God, the Father, "spared not his own Son, but delivered him up for us all." And what we claim is, that the singular emphasis laid by the sacred writers upon the death of Christ for sinners, when put side by side with the biblical doctrine of death being the divinely ordained penalty of sin, confirms our statement that his death was strictly vicarious, and was borne by him as the punishment due to those for whom he suffered.

And, secondly, the circumstance that the death of Christ is spoken of as being the death of those for whom he suffered, justifies the statement in question. If we give to the words which he employs their usual meaning, Paul writes to the Corinthians thus: "If Christ died for all, then

[1] Heb. viii. 3; ix. 12–14.

all died.[1] And the only natural explanation of this language is, that, inasmuch as the death of Christ was the punishment due to them for their sins, the claims of righteousness were met, at least conditionally, by his death; in the person of their representative and substitute they had suffered the penalty for sin prescribed by the law, and it only remained for them to accept the act of their substitute in humble faith. Weighty objections forbid any other interpretation of the apostle's language. And thus explained, it agrees with his subsequent declaration in the same chapter, that God "made him who knew no sin to be sin for us; that we might become the righteousness of God in him." An exceedingly forcible expression! In himself, as seen by the clear eye of his own perfect consciousness, Christ was sinless; yet on behalf of sinful man "he was made," not a sin-offering, nor a sinner, but, more emphatic still, "sin itself, the representative as it were of sin, the one on whom all sin was laid; that is, of course, in its destructive consequences as evil and punishment." (De Wette.) "We must remember," says Usteri on this passage, "that Paul looked upon death as the penalty of sin, and therefore the death of the sinless Christ must appear to him an assumption of *our* punish-

[1] 2 Cor. v. 15.

ment. Thus, at all events, we have found the representation of the death of Christ as vicarious to be Pauline." And Bernhard Weiss remarks on the same words of Paul: "It is here said expressly, that the treatment of the sinless as a sinner was the means whereby the treatment of sinners as sinless was made possible, and thus the new righteousness was procured on which the salvation of man depends. But the specific doom of the sinner is death, and hence the apostle rests the constraining power which the love of Christ exercises upon the judgment, that "if one died for all, then all died." The death of Christ, suffered for the salvation of men, holds as a substitute for the death of all; his treatment as a sinner makes their treatment as righteous possible, since they need not suffer again the death which he has suffered for them, and in this great act of beneficence done for them lies the constraining power of his love to them. Without such a vicarious death, the penalty of their own death could not have been remitted; for the law of God hangs the curse over all its transgressors, and this provision of the divine law must be fulfilled. From the language of the apostle's letter to the Corinthians we pass naturally to that which he uses in writing to the Galatians: "Christ redeemed us from the curse of the law, being made a curse for us."[1] And this passage confirms our interpretation of the one last considered; for the word "curse" evidently refers to the penalty of sin denounced by the law, even as the apostle had just testified: "Cursed is every one that continueth not in all things which are written in the book of the law to do them." To be made a curse is, therefore, only a more exact way of expressing the thought, to be made sin. Both refer to bearing the penalty of sin. To use the language of Weiss: "The curse rests upon him who hangeth on a tree, and Christ hung on the tree of the cross. He thus bore the curse, and inasmuch as he was himself no transgressor of the law, he became an object of the curse of the law for us, and has thereby redeemed us from this curse, so that we need no more bear it, but may now become partakers of the blessing of Abraham." It is therefore safe to affirm that these passages warrant our third statement, to wit, that Christ suffered death as the penalty due to men for their sins. But there are other and kindred forms of expression used by the sacred writers which favor the same view. Thus Peter affirms that "Christ suffered once for sins, the just for the unjust," and Paul teaches that "Christ was delivered for our offences," that "he gave himself for

[1] Gal. iii. 13.

our sins," and that "he died for our sins." Now it is well-nigh certain, almost as certain as anything can be made by language, that when the apostles wrote these sentences they had in mind actual and past sins. They were not thinking of the moral influence of Christ's death upon the hearts of sinful men, but upon the relation of that death to sins already committed. For they do not say that Christ was delivered for our regeneration, but rather for our offences. They do not teach that he died for our sanctification, but rather for our sins. And this comports with the doctrine that his suffering was vicarious. It is indeed true, that the moral influence of the Atonement on men is often mentioned along with its relation to God and the pardon of sin; but it is a fallacy too common in modern thought that such a work as the Atonement, divinely ordained and divinely accomplished, can take effect in but one direction, or be meant to reach but a single end. Such a theory is baseless.

Thirdly, the testimony of Scripture, that Christ in his death bore the sins of men, confirms the statement in question. For the phrase, "to bear sins," is used in the Old Testament figuratively, to express the idea of responsibility for them, and so of suffering the penalty which they deserve. "To feel the guilt of sin, or to bear the punishment of it," is the meaning of the phrase, according to the best authorities. Thus: "Whosoever curseth his God shall bear his iniquity" (Lev. xxiv. 15). "If a soul sin, . . . though he wist it not, yet is he guilty, and shall bear his iniquity" (Lev. v. 17). "Each day for a year shall ye bear your iniquities, even forty years" (Num. xiv. 34). Now this expression is applied to the suffering Saviour by the Epistle to the Hebrews: "Christ was once offered to bear the sins of many; and unto them that look for him shall he appear the second time without sin unto salvation (ix. 28). "To bear the sins of many" is the end here specified for which Christ, the Lamb of God, was offered in sacrifice. This was the proximate end of his death, preceding and conditioning his regal work of "giving repentance unto Israel and remission of sins," preceding also and conditioning his second advent, without the burden of sin, but glorified in his saints. The phrase before us is also used in nearly the same way by Peter: "Who his own self bare our sins in his own body on the tree" (1 Pet. ii. 24); where this act of mercy, by added clauses, is put in relation to a remoter end, the pardon and sanctification of believers, and where, accordingly, both the immediate and the ultimate end of the Atonement are contemplated. In the two passages which we have cited there is also, as the best interpreters of every school admit, an allusion to the great prophecy of the fifty-third of Isaiah, where the same expression is applied to the suffering "servant of God." It will therefore be necessary for us to look at the language of that prophecy.

This may be done most readily by quoting several sentences in a translation differing slightly from that in common use: "Surely he bore our sicknesses and carried our sorrows; and we did esteem him stricken, smitten of God, and afflicted. But he was wounded for our transgressions, crushed for our iniquities; the chastisement of our peace was upon him, and with his stripes we were healed (4, 5). Jehovah laid on him the iniquity of us all (6). By the knowledge of himself shall the Righteous One, my servant, justify many; for he himself shall bear their iniquities (11). He bore the sins of many, and made intercession for the transgressors" (12). It is not possible, if it were desirable, to put a critical exposition of these verses within the limits of our discussion; but in so far as the results to which such an exposition would lead belong to our present topic, they may be expressed in a few words. The language of Christ and of his apostles proves that the fifty-third of Isaiah was fulfilled in him. This may be regarded as certain, whether that chapter is directly

Messianic, or not; for beyond a doubt its only perfect realization was in the great Sufferer upon Calvary.

A recognition of this fact is sufficient for our present purpose, though weighty reasons, drawn from the prophecy itself and from the use made of it by the New Testament, convince us that it had from the first direct and exclusive reference to the Messiah. Taking, however, the lower ground, and only claiming what every one who receives the teaching of Christ must concede, that the language of this chapter was fulfilled in him, we call attention to certain features of this marvellous picture of the servant of Jehovah. It represents him as a great sufferer in the eyes of men; perhaps it ought to be said, as the greatest of sufferers. "His visage was so marred more than any man, and his form more than the sons of men." Behold him there, in the foreground of the picture, smitten, afflicted, despised, disease and woe pressing upon him as a heavy burden and crushing him to the earth! We see not his power, but his grief; not his victories, but his wounds; not his heroic life, but his uncomplaining death. "He is led as a lamb to the slaughter." It represents him also as being, in the eyes of men, a sufferer by the judgment of God. They believe the hand of Jehovah to be heavy upon him because of his sins. "Smitten of God and afflicted," is the language of the prophet. But when was this true of Christ, if not at his death? Was there any hour prior to that, in his earthly history, when the people thought him to be suffering under the just judgment of the Lord? The Gospels speak of none; and we must, therefore, conclude that he was set before the prophet's eye in the very hour of his death, — for then and only then, in an eminent sense, did he seem to be forsaken of God. It represents him, finally, as suffering on account of the sins of his people. Their diseases he bore, their sorrows he carried; for their transgressions he was wounded, for their iniquities he was crushed. The chastisement by which their peace was secured was laid on him. And if stronger language is demanded, the prophet adds expressly that "he bore their sins," and that "his soul made an offering for sin." That vicarious suffering was meant to be described, by these expressions, is admitted by many who reject the doctrine of the vicarious death of Christ. Bleek concedes this without hesitation; and Knobel explains the fourth verse thus: "By his sufferings he bore for us the punishments for sin which we had deserved;" also the fifth, by a similar remark: "For our salvation he bore the punishment of sin, since he satisfied the divine righteousness, and, after the atonement of sins by him, Jehovah gives back to us prosperity." On the tenth verse he adds: "Jehovah was for once pleased that his servant should be evil-entreated, and therefore he loaded him with sufferings. The writer can only explain the fact, so incongruous to human reason, that the innocent should suffer for the guilty, by referring it to the free will of God, who, as an absolute Sovereign, can do as he pleases." These comments indicate the position of this eminent rationalist on the point in question.

V. *OBJECTIONS TO THE FOREGOING VIEW.*

But an objection to our view has been drawn from the language of Matthew (viii. 17), which calls the miracles of healing wrought by Christ a fulfilment of the prophet's words: "Himself took our infirmities and bare our sicknesses." This passage of the first Gospel is brought forward by Dr. Bushnell as "being the one scriptural citation that gives, beyond a question, the *usus loquendi* of all the vicarious and sacrificial language of the New Testament." "If, then, we desire to know exactly what the substitution of Christ for sin was, and how far it went, — what it means, for example, that he bore our sins, — we have only to revert back to what is here said of his relation to sicknesses, and our question is resolved." And he proceeds to say that Christ bore our sicknesses "in the sense that he took them on his feeling, had his heart burdened by the sense of them," etc. This may be true; but Matthew does not affirm it. What he does affirm is, that Jesus "cast out the spirits with his word, and healed all that were sick." And if we must go beyond the exertion of miraculous power and suppose a deeper meaning in the words, why stop with the idea of mere sympathy? Why not be guided in our interpretation by the obvious meaning of the prophecy? Why not assume that Christ, by the holy sharpness of his vision, pierced quite through the veil of sense and natural causes to moral evil, as the black root of all disorder, the source of all suffering? Why not believe that he could heal neither bodily nor spiritual disease without a deep consciousness of his own special relation to man, as the Substitute, the Redeemer, who was to bear the penalty of a world's guilt? "Most clearly," says Preuss (Rechtfertigung, etc., p. 110), "does the retrospective effect of his blood appear from the instances where he forgave sins before his crucifixion. Did he not say to the sick of the palsy, 'Son, be of good cheer; thy sins are forgiven thee'? (Matt. ix. 2.) And to the woman who was a sinner: 'Thy sins are forgiven thee; go in peace'? (Luke vii. 48, 50.) By whose power this was effected, we well know; but on whose account did it take place? Did not Christ here, before the eyes of all, *anticipate* the fruit of his bitter death? Or, if it sufficed for forgiveness, that he came and forgave, why, then, did he die?" I would apply the same view to the passage before us, and thus explain the fact, that Matthew saw in Christ's miracles a fulfilment of Isaiah's words. I would say with another, that "Matthew saw in the benignant and merciful acts of Christ's miraculous power an anticipation of the result of his predicted suffering." So that "every cure he wrought was a visible sign that his vicarious sorrows were already effecting their object." There is nothing whatever in the language of Matthew inconsistent with the view that Christ had undertaken and already begun to bear the penalty of human sin, and therefore had authority to bear away from men all the evils which have their root in sin. And this connection between the Atonement of Christ and the miracles of healing which he wrought would fully justify the words of Matthew. We accept it as the only key which unlocks the meaning of his declaration, when the words which he quotes are seen in the light of their original context. There is one other objection to our doctrine, to the consideration of which we must now proceed.

When it is said that Christ suffered death as the

penalty due to men for their sins, the reply is often made: "Such a doctrine is incredible; for the penalty of sin is not chiefly natural death, but spiritual; not chiefly separation of body from soul, but of soul from God; it is loss of blessed fellowship with the Most High, together with a sense of his displeasure, aggravated by remorse and despair; and these Christ could not have experienced. To suppose him, the Holy, conscious of the bitterness of remorse, or the faintness of despair, or the darkness of God's wrath, is purely absurd and impossible. Hence what he bore could have been in no real sense the penalty due to men for their sins; though it may, perhaps, have been in some way a substitute for that penalty." This objection we have often met and pondered. Once it appeared to us formidable, and even insurmountable; but for a long time it has ceased to have that appearance. Yet we still look upon it as worthy of deep consideration, and shall therefore submit to the reader a few reasons for not thinking it decisive. Whether these reasons may be deemed sufficient or not, they will, it is hoped, contribute somewhat towards a just estimate of the objection, and a clear view of the whole subject.

It may then be remarked, in the first place, that this objection is not biblical, but purely rational. It rests for support on the assumed fact that remorse can only be felt for one's own sin. But this assumed fact is not self-evident; it does not belong to the small class of verities which all men are constrained by the common laws of their understanding to admit. Nor can it be established by any process of demonstration; for it pertains to the realm of actual life, in which there are mysteries and seeming contradictions unknown to the realm of pure thought. If, then, it is proved at all, it must be proved by human experience. But how can such experience make it certain? Even if it be granted that *we* are not aware of having ever felt the pangs of remorse for the sins of others, the question may still be raised: Are we sure that in our experience we have exhausted the possibilities of spiritual fellowship, and are therefore qualified to bear witness that no innocent being can so take into his own soul the remorse of a guilty brother as to realize its bitterness? Our answer to this question must be in the negative; an answer which at once refutes the plea that Christ could not have suffered the penalty due to sinners, because that penalty included a feeling of remorse. Until we are convinced, by proper evidence, that one who is innocent can in no possible way feel the spiritual pain which is justly suffered by another for his sin, the objection before us, however plausible, may be looked upon as unfounded. But if it is made to appear, on the other hand, that in some mysterious way a holy being can share the spiritual suffering actually endured by a sinner, it will not be difficult to show that such suffering may also be borne by the holy being, while it is only prospective to the sinner, and even though it be in the end turned away from the latter, so that he never suffers the penalty due to his sins. This hypothesis agrees with the biblical account of Christ's death, and we must therefore endeavor to vindicate it by further explanation from the charge of absurdity.

It may then be remarked, in the second place, that beings who have a like spiritual nature can realize and bear the spiritual sufferings of one another. By a "like spiritual nature," we mean a nature having the same essential powers and susceptibilities, though its moral condition may differ in different persons. And this "bearing another's woe" is just what is meant by sympathy and compassion, when these words are taken in their etymological and deepest sense; for they signify to suffer with another; to endure what his spirit endures; to share not his bodily ill, but the feeling which that ill excites; not his sin and guilt, but the spiritual state, the remorse and fear consequent upon them. And we maintain that this particular form of suffering is not a mere figure of speech, but a significant fact of experience. There are men who enter into a brother's sorrow, and feel it as their own, who take upon mind and heart a brother's care or doubt or fear, and bear it as truly as he does himself. And every great writer of fiction appeals to this power of the human soul. How often has the imagination of such a writer borne us away into the presence of a wounded spirit, and riveted our gaze on the inmost reality of woe! Intent upon the tragic scene, how perfectly have we lost sight of our actual condition, and made the thoughts, passions, and anxieties of a suffering brother our own! We have incorporated, for the time being, every secret of his memory and phantom of his imagination and effort of his reason, as depicted by the writer, into our spiritual life. We have suffered the anguish ascribed to him, living over again his supposed experience in our own consciousness. And could we thus go with the spirit of a friend whom we tenderly love, as it passes slowly through a period of intense suffering, — of mingled fear and shame, remorse and despair, —how complete would be the sympathy! thought repeating thought, fear palpitating with fear, pang blending with pang, and moan echoing moan, in saddest unison! But our suffering with others is kept within very narrow limits by the defectiveness of our knowledge and love. Let these be made perfect, and our sympathy might then be perfect also; but while these are partial, our sympathy will be only partial, and so not commensurate with that of Christ.

For it may now be remarked, in the third place, that Christ's human nature was perfect in knowledge and in love. Of course we do not mean to say that the human soul of Jesus had, strictly speaking, all knowledge, but merely that it had at every moment all the knowledge requisite to the complete performance of its work for that moment. And for practical ends this was as good as omniscience. Whenever he had occasion to read the thoughts of men, he needed not that any should testify of man, for he knew what was in man. Moreover, his love was equal to his knowledge, — pure, self-sacrificing, perfect. All the conditions for absolute, unrestricted sympathy met in his person. The reader may recollect, in the writings of De Quincey, an account of a child, who was rescued from drowning after she had "descended within the abyss of death and looked into its secrets as far, perhaps, as ever human eye *can* look and have permission to return. At a certain stage of this descent, a blow seemed to strike her, and a mighty theatre expanded within her brain. In a moment, in the twinkling of an eye, every act, every design, of her past life lived again; not as a succession, but as parts of a coexistence."

Thoughts, desires, passions and deeds, which, one by one, had laid themselves down to rest in the silent chambers of memory, now, as memory threw open all her doors, started up as an army of sleepers into life, and stood arrayed before the eye of her mind. Yet far less perfectly, it may be, was her own past life brought before this child in a moment of time, than was the history of every one of our race spread out before the soul of Christ in the hour of his agony. By the knowledge which Jesus possessed may all the woes of mankind in every age have been brought into his consciousness; all the restless passions, bitter memories and consuming griefs; all the fear and horror, remorse and despair, in this world or in the world to come; time past and future uniting and blending into one with the present, and arraying in a single prospect her countless souls, with all the sorrows of their experience from birth to death, and from death along the interminable line of after existence, — each throb of anguish in all the history of these sinful souls beating visibly before him, and adding its force to the rushing flood of woe which enters his heart; and by a love that was stronger than death may his soul have been knit to this great brotherhood in the fellowship of suffering, have been pierced through and through with innumerable and sharpest pangs, and have been made to stagger and almost sink, though but for an hour, under the weight of a world's woe. And as that woe includes a sense of separation from God, or rather, it may be, of his turning away in displeasure from the guilty, and leaving them to their own weakness, and darkness, and emptiness, it is not strange that Christ, entering into their experience, cried out upon the cross: "My God, my God, why hast thou forsaken me!"

Now, is there anything absurd or incredible in all this? Anything which disagrees with the known laws of spiritual life and fellowship? Anything of which there is no faintest hint or shadow in human experience? We think not. Without professing to have set forth *the way*, and the only way in which Christ actually bore the penalty due to men for their sins, — a penalty which was chiefly spiritual, including a sense of God's displeasure aggravated by remorse; without asserting or believing that Christ bore just the amount of suffering which awaited sinners unredeemed in eternity, and without overlooking the dignity of his person which gave inexpressible value to his death, we think a way has been indicated by which he *could* have borne their penal woe; and, if so, however different in some of its elements may have been the actual suffering of soul endured by Christ from what we have so feebly described, the objection to our doctrine — the doctrine that the Atonement of Christ took up into itself the penalty due to men for their sins — has been sufficiently met. Yet we are unwilling to leave the hypothesis just presented without a few additional words of explanation; especially as it has been advocated by many who deny the God-ward efficacy of the Atonement.

To begin at this point: the theory presented by us has been thought to limit the influence of Christ's sacrifice to men; thus proving itself to be simply the moral view of the Atonement in a new form. And, confessedly, it has been maintained by writers who think it involves such a limitation. But plainly it does not. For though we admit that Christ suffered by taking into his soul the experience of guilty souls, and though we admit that love to sinners enabled him to do this in harmony with the known laws of spiritual life, we do not, surely, by these admissions, deny that he consented to this fellowship in woe, because it was necessary in order to meet the claims of divine righteousness as well as to break the power of human sin. No one can read the Saviour's words, "I honor my Father;" "I do always those things that please him;" "My meat is to do the will of him that sent me, and to finish his work;" "I have glorified thee on earth;" "Father, if it be possible let this cup pass from me: nevertheless, not as I will, but as thou wilt," — without feeling that Christ was moved to drain the cup of woe by an all-controlling regard for the will and honor of God, as well as for the salvation of men. And therefore he may have been led to suffer what he did, and as he did, because that suffering would illustrate the justice of God no less than his mercy, and thus remove an obstacle to the pardon of sin.

Again, the theory presented by us favors the view that the penalty of sin is provided for in the moral constitution of the soul, and is inflicted, not chiefly by forces acting upon it from without, but by the retributive working of laws and forces within. And this may prove to be the fact. The noblest powers of our spiritual being, if perverted and outraged, may become ministers of divine justice, tormenting us for sin. And no one can imagine a more fitting or awful punishment for moral wrong than one which the moral nature, the judgment and conscience of the wrong-doer, inflicts upon him. Those who have studied most closely the capacities of man for suffering, and have scrutinized most thoroughly the language of Scripture concerning the misery of the lost, have been led, with few exceptions, to think of remorse and despair, with a sense of "what might have been," as the bitterest ingredients in the cup of woe. The sinful soul bears death in its own bosom; and therefore Milton puts these dreadful words into the mouth of Satan: —

"Which way I fly is hell; myself am hell."

Yet we cannot see how the theory in question restricts the penalty of sin to suffering which springs from the sinner's moral constitution, or forbids us to suppose that outward circumstances may enhance the misery of the lost. For all suffering occasioned by forces acting upon the soul from without must nevertheless be felt by the soul itself, and, unless new sensibilities are added hereafter to its nature, must be felt by means of those which it now possesses. But these were all possessed by Christ, and it is therefore possible that he endured every kind of suffering involved in the second death, however much of it may be occasioned by external circumstances.

At this point we close our examination of the Atonement as related to God. It has been shown, by the plain testimony of Scripture, that it removed an obstacle from the mind of God to the bestowal of renewing and pardoning grace on men; that it effected this removal by meeting in some way the claims of divine righteousness, and so exhibiting that righteousness; that it met those claims, in great part at least, by the voluntary death of Christ, which death he suffered as the penalty due to men for their sins; and that the principal objections to this view are unavailing. But while we look upon these results as fully secured by the evidence adduced from the Word of God and the soul of man, we are deeply conscious that our statement of the evidence has been very imperfect, and that we have been compelled to omit all notice of a large amount of confirmatory truth. This, however, will not be surprising to any thoughtful reader of the New Testament; for a large part of that wondrous volume has a bearing more or less direct upon the Atonement in its relations to God. Especially do we regret our inability to bring within the proper limits of this discussion a brief notice of the distinction, so often made, between the active and the passive obedience of Christ, between his perfect fulfilment of the divine law, as a rule of duty, and his voluntary submission to the penalty which it denounces against sin. But however essential a treatment of this point might be to an exhaustive work on the Atonement, it may be dispensed with in the rapid survey which we are making of this great doctrine.

And now, O Lamb of God, who didst by thy vicarious life and death meet for us the claims of divine right, in a higher and holier way than we are able fully to conceive, so that God can be just and yet justify believers in thee, be pleased to accept our thanks for thy wondrous grace, and to pardon the errors and imperfections of this attempt to set forth in human language the nature of thy sacrificial work.

CHAPTER II.

THE ATONEMENT AS RELATED TO MAN.

I. ITS MORAL INFLUENCE.

IT has been shown already that the Atonement was pre-requisite, in the order of nature, to the bestowal of renewing and forgiving grace. The gift of the Holy Spirit, by whose special action the prophets and apostles were qualified for their work, and by whose customary action the hearts of men are renewed and sanctified, was consequent in reason, if not in time, upon the death of Christ. And the same is probably true of every blessing enjoyed by men in the present life. It is by virtue of his vicarious death that we are "prisoners of hope," looking upon our salvation as possible.

But the Atonement has another and more direct relation to men, of which we are now to speak. As an exhibition of the divine character, it tends to beget sorrow for sin and trust in Christ. As a revelation of the heart of God, it moves with persuasive and subduing power upon the hearts of men. As a practical demonstration of Jehovah's love, paying homage to his righteousness, and yet reaching out its hand to recover the lost, it makes the strongest imaginable appeal to our religious nature. And this is the "moral influence" of the Atonement, — its manward efficacy, recognized by all who think the suffering of Christ of any value, and no less heartily by those who admit its Godward efficacy than by those who deny it. For plainly a love which meets the claims of divine justice, as well as the needs of sinful humanity, cannot be less sacred and powerful, as a motive, than a love which has nothing to do with the former while accomplishing the latter. If there was need of the Atonement in order that God might be just and yet justify believers in Christ, this circumstance does not diminish, but rather increases, the power of Christ's death as a motive to repentance and faith. For instance, no one will venture to pronounce the great passage in John, "God so loved the world that he gave his only-begotten Son, that whosoever believeth in him should not perish, but have everlasting life,"[1] to be a whit less effective in leading men to the exercise of faith, than it would have been if it had represented Christ as given by the Father for the purpose of leading men to believe, instead of representing him as being given for the purpose of securing eternal life to those who believe. Nay, we cannot help feeling

[1] John iii. 16.

that the latter is a far more solemn and impressive truth than the former, giving to men a much deeper view of the awful nature of sin and the boundless love of God, and exciting in them a much stronger desire to escape from evil and find peace in Christ. For whatever emphasizes the holiness and justice of God, his sense of what is due to the sinner as a fit penalty for his sins, emphasizes at the same time his love in providing a way of escape from that penalty. The greater the obstacle to be removed, the greater must be the power which removes it. The more sacred and inviolable the law of God, including its penalty, the more affecting must be the mercy of God which leads him to save the transgressor. And, if we are not mistaken, an impartial history of the Christian religion would show, beyond question, that the doctrine of a vicarious Atonement, ratifying the claims of justice, has been more effectual than any other view of the Saviour's death in convincing men of sin and leading them to him, in impressing upon their hearts both the righteousness and the love of God. And just this twofold effect is what the moral power of the Atonement ought, assuredly, to work; for this is the state of heart which the Word of God requires the sinner to have. Nay, it is a state of heart which human reason, with all its darkness, affirms that every sinner ought to have; for it is simply a proper response of the moral feelings to the deepest realities, to the moral nature of God and the moral state of man.

And we need not look beyond the New Testament for evidence of the power of the Atonement to move the religious nature of man. For the contrast between the effect of preaching before and after the death of Christ goes far to establish this fact. When, from his exaltation at the right hand of power, Christ sent the Holy Spirit at the Pentecost upon his disciples, they began for the first time to preach the gospel with marked success; and this success, though due in part to a wonderful outpouring of the Spirit, was certainly due in a great measure to the saving truth which was now preached with unprecedented clearness. Christ was lifted up before men, and never had the law of God appeared to them so holy, or sin so culpable, as in the light streaming from his cross. Their hearts were pierced with a sense of guilt, and they cried aloud for mercy. The words of Bernard in his Bampton Lectures are exactly in point: "Men have sometimes expressed their wonder at this difference in the effect of the Lord's own preaching and of that of his disciples; and they have been fain to ascribe it to the outpouring of the Spirit, which wrought a sudden change in the hearts of the hearers. But we have no encouragement to suppose that the three thousand who believed on the day of Pentecost received any *special* gift of the Spirit (such as originated on that day) until *after* they believed. This was promised by the apostle as a gift, not preceding, but ensuing on their baptism. The true reason for the change in the effect of the doctrine is found in the change which had passed upon the doctrine itself. Only when it is possible freely and fully to publish the one 'name under heaven given among men, whereby they must be saved,' are their consciences thoroughly roused and their trust decisively secured."

We may also in this connection refer to the language of Paul in describing the Gospel which he proclaimed. Writing to the Corinthians, he says: "We preach Christ crucified, unto the Jews a stumbling-block and unto the Greeks foolishness, but unto them which are called . . Christ the power of God and the wisdom of God;"[1] and in another paragraph of the same letter: "I determined not to know anything among you, save Jesus Christ, and him crucified."[1] In a second epistle to the same church, he gives apparently the substance of what he was wont to preach in the following words: "We pray you in Christ's stead, be ye reconciled to God. For he made him to be sin for us, who knew no sin, that we might be made the right-

[1] 1 Cor. i. 23, 24. [2] 1 Cor. ii. 2.

eousness of God in him." The same kind of message is also implied in his exclamation to the Galatians: "Who hath bewitched you, that ye should not obey the truth, before whose eyes Christ was evidently set forth [by my preaching], crucified among you?"[1] It is certain, from such expressions as these, that the preaching of Paul had for its principal theme, not the holy life, but the atoning death of Christ. Upon this he relied as the argument most likely to reach the conscience and the heart, whether of the unbeliever or of the believer. Recognizing the Saviour's character as perfect, he nevertheless appealed to his propitiatory suffering as the strongest motive to repentance. And this reveals to us his estimate of the moral power of the Atonement; an estimate which cannot wisely be called in question. For, to say nothing of his profound knowledge of the human heart, of his eager desire to lead men to Christ, of his readiness to become all things to all men that he might save some, of his care for the churches and zeal for the progress of believers in sanctification,—to say nothing of these facts as giving weight to his judgment on such a point as the one before us, there is a still higher reason for our accepting it as final, namely, the fact that, having received the Gospel by revelation from Christ, he was guided in the work of preaching it by the Holy Spirit. We may, there-

[1] Gal. iii. 1.

fore, be certain, that he made principal use of such Christian truth as was best fitted in its nature to reach the hearts of men and win them to the Saviour. And that truth, as his own words declare, was the doctrine of Christ crucified.

There are also several expressions in the Word of God which may be supposed to ascribe moral purification to the direct influence of the Atonement. Thus John speaks of "the blood of Jesus Christ as cleansing those who walk in the light from all sin,"[1] and ascribes eternal glory and dominion "unto Him that loved us and washed us from our sins in his own blood."[2] And Peter refers to Christ as "bearing our sins in his own body on the tree, that we, being dead to sins, should live unto righteousness; by whose stripes ye were healed."[3] But it may be urged that all these expressions, except the first, carry back the mind to a work completed in some past time, as at the death of Christ, while the moral influence of the Atonement is continuous, reaching down in the case of every Christian to the present time, and almost certain to be described by verbal forms answering to this fact. To such an objection we can reply, that the sacred writers may have had in mind simply and exclusively the moral influence of Christ's death at the time of regeneration. Yet this does not seem to be a natural explanation of their language, which more probably refers to the

[1] 1 John i. 7. [2] Rev. i. 5. [3] 1 Peter ii. 24.

indirect working of the Atonement. But what shall be said of the first passage quoted, namely, "The blood of Jesus Christ, his Son, cleanseth us from all sin"? It has respect, we think, to the direct moral influence, or sanctifying power, of the cross; as may also the language of the Epistle to the Hebrews: "How much more shall the blood of Christ, who through the eternal Spirit offered himself without spot to God, purge your conscience from dead works to serve the living God!"[1] And the words of Ebrard are not too strong: "Whoever has a living faith in the atoning death of Christ, cannot love the sin which brought him to the cross. And therefore the blood of Jesus exerts a continuous purifying influence, until it has cleansed the heart from all sin. But his blood and death have this power, because he was and is *the Son of God*, in whom the Father was revealed."

All that remains to be said on the moral influence of the Atonement is but an expansion of this last remark. For the wonderful power of Christ's death over the hearts of men is certainly due to the revelation which it made of the mind of God. A moment's reflection will satisfy every one of this. Moreover, the revelation of the divine mind made by the Saviour's death was due to the union of deity and humanity in his person. It could not have been made by him as a mere man,

[1] Heb. ix. 14.

though living without sin and suffering a martyr's death. For as a man simply, he must have been subject and finite, unable to stand in God's place and represent adequately in conduct his feeling. He might indeed have shown very clearly how much God would have a subject of his moral government do or suffer for the benefit of others, but not how much the Supreme Ruler would be pleased himself to do or suffer for such an end. Yet it is this which the heart of man longs to know; it is the latter, and not the former, which will touch the deepest chords of his spiritual nature. And as Christ was the brightness of the Father's glory, the express image of his being, and therefore able to say, He that hath seen me hath seen the Father; moreover, as in him dwelt all the fulness of the Godhead bodily, and he could pronounce his own words to be, in deepest reality, the Father's words, and his own works to be inseparable from his Father's working, so likewise did his suffering reveal, in the clearest and surest manner possible, the inmost heart of God, his infinite regard for right and his infinite love to men. Or, resuming the language which we have already used, the vicarious death of Christ, as a practical demonstration of Jehovah's love, paying homage to righteousness and yet reaching out its hand to recover the lost, makes the strongest imaginable appeal to the religious nature of man. This attitude of his Maker towards him is inexpressibly moving. It will do all that moral influence can do to melt the stubborn spirit of rebellion, and lead the sinner to cry for pardon. There is a deep meaning in the apostle's words: "We love him because he first loved us;" for it is the tendency of love to beget love; and, if any truth could by its own proper influence originate spiritual life in a sinful soul, it would be the truth, so often repeated in the New Testament, that Christ suffered for sins, the just for the unjust, to bring us to God; for this truth presents the highest instance, the crowning manifestation of divine love to men. "He that spared not his own Son, but delivered him up for us all, how shall he not with him also freely give us all things?"

And if it is but too evident, that no amount of light, even though it reveal infinite love as well as holiness in God, will of itself, without the renewing action of the Spirit, lead a sinner to repentance, still it is to be remembered that the fault is not in the light, nor in the character of God which it reveals, but in the sinner's evil heart and stubborn will. What if the soul must be made sensitive to the light by the Spirit, yet it is the light which, poured in upon the soul, originates the image of Christ, the new life of faith and love. If it is the direct action of the Spirit which prepares the plate, it is the direct influence of truth which brings out the picture. And there is no light so clear, no truth so potent for this wondrous work, as that which beams from the cross. Besides, it should never be forgotten, that while the death of Christ, as made known to us by the Scriptures, conveys to the heart the most precious and subduing truth of religion, it also procures the action of the Holy Spirit in the heart to prepare it for the working of truth. Thus all grace flows from the cross, and the Godward efficacy of the Atonement increases its manward efficacy. No wonder, then, that it has been the chief theme of the greatest preachers in every age! No wonder that from Apollos to Spurgeon it has filled the hearts and kindled the eloquence of faithful men! No human intellect is large enough to comprehend the spiritual good which has emanated from the suffering of Gethsemane and Calvary.

II. EXTENT OF THE ATONEMENT.

We have spoken more than once of the "manward or moral" influence of the Atonement, as if these two adjectives were nearly equivalent, at least for the purposes of the present discussion. In one respect, however, this is by no means the case. For, as the phrase is commonly used, the moral influence of the Atonement is limited to those who have some knowledge of Christ's death, such knowledge being the only channel by which, in the form of moral influence, his love and compassion are brought to bear upon their spiritual state. But the manward influence of the Atonement is far more extensive. It comprises all the good which reaches men in any way as the fruit of the Saviour's death. And this good includes the renovating and sanctifying work of the Spirit, without which the moral power of the Redeemer's suffering would fail of bringing a single soul to God. It also includes the salvation of all the elect who, dying in infancy, are regenerated by the simple action of the Holy Spirit, without a knowledge of Christian truth. And it probably includes all the blessings which the non-elect enjoy on earth. The relation of the Atonement to man is therefore far more extensive than its moral influence.

But this wider reach or relation can be ascribed to its manward efficacy only on the ground of its Godward efficacy. For if it has no influence on the mind or government of God, it cannot condition the work of his Spirit; and then, what remains but simply the moral influence of Christ's life moving men to repentance? An influence which is restricted, by the nature of the case, to those who have the Gospel! An influence which does not touch those who die in infancy, nor those who may have believed in God, without a knowledge of Christ and him crucified! How many there have been of the latter class we know not; but if any of the ancient Israelites were led to faith in God, by the concurrent action of his Spirit on their hearts, of the Mosaic law convicting them of sin, and of the Levitical sacrifices teaching them God's mercy, their salvation, according to this view, was due in no respect to the death of Christ; for the story of his dying love was unknown to them, and could not, therefore, in the way of moral influence, lead them to God. His name is not the name, his work is not the work, by which they were saved. But we have shown that the Atonement has a most important effect on the divine mind and government, — a Godward influence of the highest moment, — and it is therefore logical as well as scriptural to trace all the good which men have in this life to the work of Christ. Especially must we trace to that work the agency of the Holy Spirit in forming the heart anew and preparing it for holy action. Hence the manward efficacy of the Atonement is far more extensive than its direct moral influence; and it is so, because the Atonement has also a Godward power and working.

Looking, then, at the extent of the Atonement

as related to men, we may say, *in the first place*, that it was intended to secure the salvation of all the elect. For while it removed an obstacle, in the divine mind, to their forgiveness upon repentance, it also procured for them the Holy Spirit to work in their hearts that repentance. The whole economy of grace rests manifestly on the vicarious death of Christ, and therefore all divine influences, whether directly or indirectly from the Spirit, are results of that death. But these influences are such as will bring all the elect into spiritual union with Christ, and, by keeping alive their faith in him, preserve them to eternal glory. For the language of Bernard is not too strong: "Believers are in Christ, so as to be partakers in all that he does, and has, and is. They died with him, and rose with him, and live with him, and in him are seated in heavenly places. When the eye of God looks on them, they are found in Christ, and there is no condemnation to them that are in him, and they are righteous in his righteousness, and loved with the love which rests on him, and are sons of God in his sonship, and heirs with him of his inheritance, and are soon to be glorified with him in his glory. And this standing which they have in Christ, and the present and future portion which it secures, are contemplated in eternal counsels, and predestined before the foundation of the world."

In further support of our statement it may be remarked, that the fact of personal election proves that Christ suffered on the cross to ensure the salvation of all the elect; the fact that God made choice, from the beginning, of the persons who were to have eternal life through the death of his Son, is evidence enough that he had special regard to their life in the gift of that Son. The two go together. For the ends to be reached by the use of certain means will assuredly be kept in view by him who uses intelligently the given means. And, therefore, as believers were "predestinated according to the purpose of Him who worketh all things after the counsel of his own will,"[1] their salvation must have been sought, as a definite and glorious end, in making the Atonement. In harmony with this view, the apostle speaks of the saints as those "who were chosen in Christ before the foundation of the world,"[2] and as those who were "called according to the purpose and grace of God, which was given them in Christ Jesus before the world began,"[3] — passages which teach us that the election of grace, and the grace which follows election, are connected, in the mind of God, with Christ and him crucified, as their procuring cause, or essential condition. The electing grace of God has its

[1] Eph. i. 2. [2] Eph. i. 4. [3] 1 Tim. i. 9.

ground in the redeeming work of Christ, — and the former could never have been exercised without the latter. But there are even clearer expressions of this truth in the Word of God. For, according to the fourth Gospel, Christ represents himself more than once as the Good Shepherd, who lays down his life for the sheep; and the sheep he characterizes as those who hear his voice and follow him, to whom he gives eternal life, and whom none can pluck out of his hand. And just before he sought retirement in the garden for his great agony, he said of his disciples: "I pray for them. I pray not for the world, but for them which thou hast given me; for they are thine. Neither pray I for these alone, but for them also which shall believe on me through their word."[1] It is natural to suppose that in suffering, as well as in prayer, he had a peculiar regard for his own, for the sheep whom he laid down his life to save. Moreover, the evangelist informs us that Jesus died, not for the "nation only, but also to gather together in one the children of God that were scattered abroad;" and Paul declares that "Christ loved the church and gave himself for it." But it is needless to multiply citations. For it is plain that God purposed from the first to save certain persons of our race; that these persons were given to Christ in a special sense, to be his flock, and

[1] John xvii. 9, 20.

that he had particularly in view their actual salvation when he laid down his life. Thus far, at least, it would seem as if there could be no question as to the sense of Scripture.

But this is not all. We are taught by the Word of God to say, *in the second place*, that the Atonement was meant by its Author to be a provision for the salvation of every man who would repent. In other words, it put out of the way every obstacle to universal pardon, except that of unbelief. And in this sense Christ died for all; not only was his expiatory suffering a sufficient reason for the pardon of all mankind, in case of repentance, but it was meant to be this. Such we suppose to be the teaching of Scripture; and that teaching must be accepted as final. But as some, whom we love in the Gospel, do not find this doctrine in the Sacred Record, it may be well to look at a few passages thought to contain it.

One of them reads thus: "But there were false prophets also among the people, even as there will be false teachers among you, who will bring in privily destructive factions, even denying the Lord who bought them, bringing upon themselves swift destruction."[1] This language certainly appears to teach that some of those whom Christ bought with his own blood will finally perish. But Mr. Symington believes that a different view of it is tenable.

[1] 2 Peter ii. 1.

The apostle, he says, "argues against them on their own principles, and shows that their conduct was heinous and dangerous in the extreme. And in so doing he only follows the example of the Saviour himself, who confuted the Pharisees, who professed to be righteous and were not, on their own acknowledged principles: 'I say unto you that likewise joy shall be in heaven over one sinner that repenteth, more than over ninety and nine just persons which need no repentance.' Are we to conclude, from this, that there were any such just persons who needed no repentance? Surely not." Very well, so far as the language of Christ is concerned. But the language of Peter is no parallel to that of Jesus; for the latter had taught expressly that the Pharisees were *not* righteous, but, on the contrary, were self-righteous, hypocritical, oppressive, and offensive to God. No one, therefore, could for a moment suppose that he meant to call them truly righteous. But Peter has nowhere said, distinctly and repeatedly, that the non-elect were *not* bought with the blood of Christ. This makes all the difference in the world between the language of Christ and that of Peter, and destroys the force of Mr. Symington's argument from the former to the latter. We come back, then, to the obvious meaning of the apostle's testimony, and conclude that some for whom Christ shed his blood upon the cross will perish at last.

And if he died for some who will perish, it may safely be inferred that he died for all. Nor can it be said that his intention was in part defeated; for his atoning death was not, strictly speaking, meant to effect the salvation of all, but to remove any obstacle existing outside of their own hearts to their salvation; and this was fully accomplished. Thus, while Christ became, by his vicarious suffering, the Saviour of all men, he became in a still more eminent sense the Saviour of them that believe.

But the fact which is fairly implied in the words of Peter seems to be directly affirmed by the Apostle John: "And if any man sin, we have an advocate with the Father, Jesus Christ the righteous. And he is the propitiation for our sins; and not for ours only, but also for the whole world."[1] Here the sins of believers are contrasted with those of the world; and the propitiatory death of Christ is said to have respect, not to the former only, but also to the latter. Moreover, as the word propitiation refers to the sacrificial death of Christ, it is distinguishable from redemption, since it does not imply an actual deliverance from wrath. For when the Jewish high priest, on the great day of Atonement, made reconciliation for all the people, a way was opened for them to come before God with acceptance; but if they refused to

[1] John ii, 2.

do this and despised his service, his indignation still burned against them. The same is true of Christ. He was set forth as a propitiation, to exhibit the righteousness of God, in order that God might be just while justifying the believer in Jesus. And even if the word "Advocate" has reference to believers only, the word "propitiation" may well have a wider reference; for the apostle's thought may be thus expressed: "My little children, I write these things to you, that ye may not sin. But I do not forget what I have just said, that no one of us has avoided every sin. Yet the Christian, who has fallen into sin, need not despair of pardon; for though, as transgressors, we cannot come ourselves before a holy God, we have an advocate with him, even Jesus Christ who is righteous, and who evermore intercedes for us. And this he can do with far greater effect than the Jewish high priest, who entered the holy of holies with another's blood, for he comes with his own blood, an ample basis for his plea in our behalf, since it was offered by him as a suitable expiation for our sins, and indeed not for ours only, but for the sins of all mankind, our own included." This view of the apostle's thought is favored by the word "whole," prefixed to "world,"—the "whole world," meaning all mankind, without exception.

Moreover, the doctrine of Paul agrees with that of Peter and John. For he speaks of the Saviour as One "who gave himself a ransom for all, to be testified in due time;"[1] and we infer, from the context, that he means all men, and not all the elect. For in the verse which begins the paragraph containing the words quoted by us, the apostle exhorts that prayer be made for "all men;" an expression which we dare not restrict to all classes of men, that is, to the elect from all nations and orders of men, but must take in its largest sense, as signifying all mankind, without exception. Nor do we find any objection to this view in the reason which is given for such prayer, namely, that it is acceptable to God, "who desires that all men should be saved and come to the knowledge of the truth;" for, by the order of the Greek words, we know that the stress falls, not upon "desires," nor upon "be saved," but upon "all men." Paul asserts that we should pray for all men, not because God *greatly desires* their salvation, but because God desires that *all men* should be saved. Of course there is a difference between desire and purpose. And if any one is in doubt whether God can be truly said to desire, in any sense, the salvation of all mankind, let him ponder his words by Ezekiel: "I have no

[1] 1 Tim. ii. 6.

pleasure in the death of him that dieth, saith the Lord God; but turn ye and live;" and the no less weighty exclamation of Christ: "Jerusalem, Jerusalem, that killest the prophets and stonest them which are sent unto thee, how often would I have gathered thy children together, even as a hen gathereth her chickens under her wings, and ye would not!"

Without appealing to other passages in the Sacred Record, we feel ourselves authorized to say, that the vicarious suffering of Christ was intended to be an ample basis or reason for the pardon of all mankind, should they believe in Jesus. It is such a basis, not simply because it must be so, on account of the infinite dignity and worth of the Sufferer, but also because it was the eternal desire and purpose of God to remove from every sinner's path the only obstacle to his salvation, except his own impenitence and unbelief. In so far the Atonement was designed for all men, and may be preached with absolute sincerity to them, as a full and perfect ground of acceptance, if they will believe.

PART THIRD.

THE "VICARIOUS SACRIFICE" OF DR. BUSHNELL.

PART THIRD.

"THE VICARIOUS SACRIFICE" OF DR. BUSHNELL.

CHAPTER I.

THE FUNDAMENTAL PRINCIPLES OF DR. BUSHNELL'S WORK.

I. GENERAL CHARACTERISTICS.

THIS production is equally remarkable in thought, in spirit, and in expression.

It exhibits great boldness of speculative thought, laying hold of the root-questions of theology and attempting to construct a philosophy of the moral universe. As Dr. Hickok, in his "Rational Cosmology," tells us how the natural universe must have been made and therefore was made, so Dr. Bushnell tells us, in "The Vicarious Sacrifice," how the moral universe is governed and must be governed. To do this one must indeed have a vast amount of knowledge; but the writer seems to be sure of himself on this point, never intimating the presence of a doubt in his own mind as to anything in the heavens above or in the earth beneath which relates to his theme. To illustrate this remark we may refer to his language in respect to Martin Luther. If there is any doctrine which Luther distinctly conceived and believed, it was the doctrine of justification through the imputed righteousness of Christ, or, to use the skilfully chosen words of Dr. Bushnell, it was "the fact that an innocent being had taken his sins and evened the account of justice by suffering their punishment." This he believed with all his mind, and soul, and strength. How any who are familiar with his writings can entertain a doubt of this is incomprehensible. Yet the author of "The Vicarious Sacrifice" uses the following language: "This he thought he believed; but we are not obliged to believe that he did. Really believing it, and conceiving what it means, the fact would have set his stout frame shuddering and turned his life to gall. The truth indeed appears to be, that his heart sailed over his theology, and did not come down to see it. . . . Let no one be surprised, then, that Luther's justification by faith, that which puts his soul ringing with such an exultant and really sublime liberty, makes a plunge so bewildering into bathos and general unreason, when it comes to be affirmed theologically in his doctrine. As he had it in his Christian consciousness, the soul of his joy, the rest of his confidence, the enlargement of his gracious liberty, nothing could be more evidently real and related to the deepest necessities of feeling; but as he gave it in his dogmatic record, I confess that calling it justification by faith, — *articula stantis vel cadentis ecclesiæ*, — I could more easily see the church fall than believe it." There is an air of independent smartness about this last expression which may please the fancy, but it seems to us wanting in a certain quality of reverence and modesty which adorned the language of Christ and his apostles. Still the most striking feature of this extract is the writer's claim to know what Martin Luther had in his consciousness better than Luther himself knew. For it is most certain, that the doctrine of justification by faith, as the great German reformer had it in his Christian consciousness, "put his soul ringing with an exultant and really sublime liberty," and he distinctly, repeatedly, and with all reasonable clearness and vigor of speech, describes the doctrine which thus electrified his soul with joy;[1]

[1] This will appear from a few sentences in his Commentary on the Galatians, e. g.: "For he (Paul) saith not, that Christ was made a curse for himself, but for us. Therefore all the weight of the matter standeth in his word 'for us.' For Christ is innocent as concerning his own person, and therefore he ought not to have been hanged upon a tree." . . "We are sinners and thieves, and therefore guilty of death and eternal damnation. . . . Christ took all our sins upon him, and for them died upon the cross. . . . And this, no doubt, all the prophets did foresee in spirit, that Christ should

but Dr. Bushnell is pleased to say that Luther did not know what he really believed, that his doctrine, formally stated, was mere "bathos" and "unreason," and that "his heart sailed over his theology, and did not come down to see it." On the same principle, he must say this also of Calvin and

become the greatest trangressor, murderer, adulterer, thief, rebel, and blasphemer, that ever was or could be in the world. For he, being made a sacrifice for the sins of the whole world, is not now an innocent person and without sins, . . but a sinner, which hath and carrieth the sin of Paul, who was a blasphemer, an oppressor, and a persecutor; of Peter, which denied Christ; of David, which was an adulterer, a murderer, and caused the Gentiles to blaspheme the name of the Lord," etc. (pp. 338-9.) "He verily was innocent, because he is the unspotted and undefiled Lamb of God. But because he beareth the sins of the world, his innocency is burdened with the sins and guilt of the whole world. Whatsoever sins I, thou, and we all have done, or shall do hereafter, they are Christ's own sins, as verily as if he himself had done them. To be brief, our sin must needs become Christ's own sin, or else we shall perish forever." "Wherefore Christ was not only crucified and died, but sin also (through the love of the divine Majesty) was laid upon him. When sin was laid upon him, then cometh the law, and saith, Every sinner must die. Therefore, O Christ, if thou wilt answer, become guilty, and suffer punishment for sinners, thou must also bear sin and malediction. . . And this is a singular consolation for all Christians, so to clothe Christ in our sins, and to wrap him in my sins, thy sins, and the sins of the whole world, and so to behold him bearing all our iniquities. . . If it be so that we put away sin by the works of the law and charity, then Christ taketh them not away. For if he be the Lamb of God ordained from everlasting to take away the sins of the world; and moreover, if he be so wrapped in our sins that he became accursed for us, it must needs follow that we cannot be justified by works. For God hath laid our sins, not upon us, but upon his Son Christ, that he, bearing the punishment thereof, might be our peace." (pp. 360-1.) "So, making a happy exchange with us, he took upon him our sinful person, and gave unto us his innocent and victorious person, wherewith we being now clothed, are freed from the curse of the law. . . This image and this mirror we must have continually before us, and behold the same with a steadfast eye of faith. He that doth so hath this innocency and victory of Christ, although he be never so great a sinner." (p. 365.)

Knox, of Bunyan and Edwards, of Fuller and Chalmers. And it may be true; but if so, the lessons of history are worthless; for no reason can be given for thinking that Martin Luther or Jonathan Edwards drew less comfort from the Gospel than does Horace Bushnell, or that they apprehended less distinctly the doctrines which gave them comfort.

The spirit of Dr. Bushnell, as revealed in this book, is bold and earnest. He writes like one who has an important message to deliver, and is resolved to do it effectually. He speaks out the faith that is in him without fear or favor, — vehemently, indeed, yet shrewdly, — and the tone of his work will not only attract, but also convince, many who would not be reached by a less confident faith, or a less ardent zeal. To this spirit we cannot object. Boldness and zeal in defending truth are always admirable, and it is a difficult task to criticise them even when they animate the defenders of error. But "The Vicarious Sacrifice" does not teach error simply. Noble sentiments and Christian views abound in the work. It sets forth with captivating freshness and power the nature of true benevolence, and deepens our sense of its marvellous working in the mind of God. It asserts boldly and truly, if not always on the basis of correct interpretation, the equal love of the Father and the Holy Spirit with the Son to our fallen race. It proclaims the deity of Christ with triumphant voice, though possibly from the stand-point of Sabellius. It asserts the deep depravity of man and his moral helplessness, giving due emphasis to God's grace in working a change in his spiritual state. It stirs, inspires, and elevates the soul by some of its utterances, and makes one feel the grandeur of life.

In expression the work is also remarkable. The language, always forcible and sometimes beautiful, is in many passages sublime, rising majestically with the thought and rolling on like waves of the ocean. Yet, with all its great qualities, the style of this treatise is not, in our opinion, well adapted to secure the proper ends of theological discussion. It is too intense, too impassioned; not sufficiently exact and judicial. A style like that of Mansel, or Mozley, or McCosh, calm, clear, and logical, would have added much to the value of the work. We do not say that the author could have written after this manner, but we believe that this manner is far preferable to his for such a discussion, and that, if he could not attain it, he is wanting in certain mental and spiritual qualities very necessary to a Christian philosopher. The style of Dr. Bushnell, in "The Vicarious Sacrifice," is essentially that of a reformer. He writes fervidly, powerfully, as if to carry a point by enlisting the feelings of his reader; not accurately, calmly, weighing his thoughts and words in a balance, as if the truth might be trusted to stand by its own strength and shine by its own light. This may be simply the result of a fervid mental and moral state at the time of writing, and we partly believe it is; yet there are instances of a resort to caricature in setting forth the views of other men which weaken, though they do not destroy, this explanation. The thought has more than once been suggested, that the writer is not always borne along by the deep current and flow of logical conviction, but is sometimes moving heaven and earth to carry a point with his reader. Yet this thought, we are willing to believe, is not confirmed by the work as whole. But we turn from this line of criticism to the doctrinal contents of the work.

II. THE NATURE OF THE MORAL LAW.

It is very important to ascertain, if possible, the central or radical principle of right. If there is such a principle underlying all forms of duty, it must give unity and coherence to the moral law in detail, and a knowledge of it must precede a scientific treatment of ethics. Dr. Bushnell speaks on this point as follows: "In the positive statute,

Thou shalt love the Lord thy God, and thy neighbor as thyself, there was really something fundamental; it was in fact the law of laws." (255.) Again: "The necessary and absolute law of right is very nearly answered by the relational law of love; so that any realm of being compacted in right will as certainly be unified in love, doing and suffering, each for each, just what the most self-immolating, dearest love requires." At first, then, Dr. Bushnell pronounces the absolute law of right to be nearly equivalent to the relational law of love, and obedience to the one to be always conjoined with obedience to the other. But as he goes on, and his mind becomes heated or clarified by the discussion, he becomes more positive. "Righteousness, translated into a word of the affections, is love, and love, translated back into a word of the conscience, is righteousness."[1] Again: "The eternal law of right . . . is only another conception of the law of love." "The two principles, right and love, appear to exactly measure each other." (306.)

According to Dr. Bushnell, then, the sum total of duty is love. But what does he mean by love? This question must be answered before we can have an

[1] Several of these passages were transcribed from the first edition of the work without marking the pages; the writer has not that edition at hand, and is therefore unable to supply the references.

exact view of his doctrine. Does he mean by it a benevolence which is without discrimination, having no regard to natural worth or capacity, but merely seeking the happiness of its object? Or does he mean by it a benevolence which, while having regard to natural worth, has no respect to moral character, being equally strong whether its object is holy or sinful, an angel or a fiend? Or does he mean by it an affection which is graduated by the worth of its object, which is stronger to the good than to the evil, and strongest to Him who is greatest and best? To these questions he has given no distinct reply.

But we cannot suppose that he uses the term "love" in the first sense specified, that is, to denote a benevolence which has no regard to natural worth or capacity; for, in that case, God might be said to love a worm as much as a man. This view of love severs it from reason and makes it a mere instinct. For it is plain that a benevolence under law to reason must desire the happiness of different beings, when other things are equal, in proportion to their capacity for enjoyment. The happiness of two beings of the same order must be twice as valuable as that of one, and just as valuable as that of a single being whose capacity is equal to that of both. If it be said, that parental love is not graduated by the natural worth of its objects, because the idiot child is cherished with as much affection as the one of greatest promise, it may be replied that parental love is mainly an instinct; that it is under law to divine and not to human knowledge; that many an idiot may have a spiritual nature of largest measure, capable of vast enjoyment in a future state, and therefore worthy of the highest love from the Omniscient One as well as from those who love by virtue of an instinct received from him. Hence, we are unable to say that the proper action of benevolence, as a moral affection, may be inferred from the action of parental love. Nor can we believe that a woman who is as anxious to promote the comfort of her lap-dog as of her human servant is an illustration of the wise and holy benevolence of God.

Again, it is difficult for us to believe that Dr. Bushnell uses the term "love" in the second sense specified above, that is, to denote a benevolence which, while having regard to natural worth, has no respect to moral character, but is equally strong whether its object be holy or sinful. Can it be maintained seriously that our desire for the welfare of Satan ought to be as strong as our desire for that of Gabriel? Can it be truly said that capacity is of more account than character in fixing the measure of benevolence which we should feel to a moral being? Such a view will not find favor with an enlightened conscience. No one can suppose that God loves the enemy of all good as deeply as he loves the humblest angel who kept his first estate; nor can any one believe that we ought to love God with all the heart, simply because he is the greatest being, and not also because he is the best. While we are exhorted to do good unto all, the apostle adds a sentence pertinent to the question in debate, namely, "especially to those who are of the house hold of faith." Was this added because believers have greater natural powers than unbelievers? No indication of such a reason is to be found in the Sacred Record. Again, Christ says to his disciples, "Whosoever doeth the will of my Father, the same is my brother, and sister, and mother,"—language which seems to recognize moral character as the basis of love. Besides, sin if persisted in must diminish gradually the sinner's capacity for happiness, and by so much at least the love which ought to be felt for him. This appears to be a self-evident truth, though it may be nowhere taught in the Scriptures, and though the passages to which reference has been made suggest another reason for the diminished love which is felt for sinners. In a word, we accept the hypothesis of Bishop Butler, as not merely an expression of his own opinion, but also of the truth itself on the point in question: "Perhaps divine goodness, with which, if I mistake not, we make very free in our speculations, may not be a bare single disposition to produce happiness; but a disposition to make the good, the faithful, the honest, happy. Perhaps an infinitely perfect mind may be pleased with seeing his creatures behave suitably to the nature which he has given them; to the relations which he has placed them in to each other; and to that which they stand in to himself; that relation to himself, which, during their existence, is ever necessary, and which is the most important of all: perhaps, I say, an infinitely perfect mind may be pleased with this moral piety of moral agents, *in and for itself;* as well as upon account of its being essentially conducive to the happiness of his creation."

But if Dr. Bushnell uses the term "love," in the third sense, to denote an affection which is graduated by the worth of the object, all things considered, and is therefore stronger to the good than to the evil, it is easy to see that the love of God to his creatures must vary in degree with their moral character. He will love moral beings in proportion to their moral excellence, for this is their noblest quality, and must therefore do more than any other to determine the degree of his love. Hence, too, the love of God to a moral being must diminish when such a being chooses evil instead of good, and must reach its *minimum* when the latter passes beyond the utmost limits of recovery and gives itself up to "eternal sin;" when its glorious possibilities of rectitude and blessedness cease forever. God can feel no approbation for the character nor desire for the recovery of such a being; for approbation would be absurd and desire vain. But may not God sympathize with such a being in its ruin, even though he has no desire on the whole for its recovery? May he not forever regret its fall, deploring the loss of possible good and the bitterness of actual woe which it suffers? May not love take the form of pure sorrow, unmingled with wrath, for the offender? This we imagine to be Dr. Bushnell's view of the case; for such a view is required by his theory that, in the last analysis, righteousness and love are one and the same. But it does not seem to us satisfactory. It expresses at best only a part of the truth. For incorrigible sinners are abhorred as well as pitied by the righteous Jehovah. His displeasure burns against them as destroyers of that in which he delights. Indeed, they are more guilty than miserable, and more to be blamed than to be pitied. This appears to be the uniform testimony of the Word of God; and no ethical theory will stand against that testimony, for in the end the Word of

God is always supported by conscience. Moreover, if God is pleased with a right moral character as such, he must be displeased with a wrong one; for they are opposites. To love holiness is to hate sin, and to love sin is to hate holiness. In this remark we have in view the qualities themselves, and not their fruits; for only the former are personal and have to do with love to persons. But if it is right, other things being equal, to love a holy being better than a sinful one; if, moreover, the degree of love should be regulated chiefly by the moral worth of its object; and if love of moral integrity is in its very nature hatred of moral perversity and wrong, — then clearly a moral being may become so utterly lost to good and given up to evil, that God's aversion to his character may overbalance any regard due to the original worth of his nature, any regret that misery instead of joy is its final portion. Hence justice may be right as well as grace, wrath as well as love. If Christian love is not simply a benevolent instinct, a desire for the happiness of sentient being without regard to moral character; if it is an affection strengthened by the virtue and enfeebled by the sin of its object, then it is evident that righteousness cannot be resolved into love; for the righteousness of God to all his creatures must be equal, invariable, while his love is variable. In other words, there must be evermore in him a *maximum* of righteousness towards even the most abandoned rebel, though there may be but a *minimum* of love. This representation accords with the language of Scripture and with the verdict of conscience.

Furthermore, as it seems to us, the theory that righteousness is identical with benevolence leads to the conclusion thus boldly expressed by Dr. Dwight: "Virtue is founded in utility. . . There is no ultimate good but happiness. . . Virtue is the original cause of happiness. . . Were sin in its own proper tendency to produce, invariably, the same good which it is the tendency of virtue to produce, the same glory to God, the same enjoyment to the universe, no reason is apparent to me why it would not be excellent, commendable, and rewardable, in the same manner as virtue now is." On the contrary, we believe that virtue is commendable in itself, and vice reprehensible in itself, entirely apart from the consequences of either. We hold that our moral judgment approves truth and love as better *per se* than falsehood and malice. The decision, however, is an ultimate one, admitting of no reason for it but the moral nature of God reflected in our own. Hence the mistake of Dr. Dwight and of others belonging to the same school in theology. They must needs have a reason why right is right, and wrong is wrong; and the only reason which they can imagine is the tendency of one to increase, and of the other to diminish, the happiness of the universe. But the fact appears to be that moral excellence is good in itself; a high and holy quality of soul which is worthy of admiration and reward, and which God, who presides over the universe, will in the end reward with happiness inconceivable. If, then, the theory that righteousness and love are one and the same leads to the view that happiness is the only good, and utility the ultimate ground of right, this result is an objection to the theory itself.

But there is a stronger objection; for it may be shown by a simple illustration that righteousness is not identical with benevolence. Suppose that A has in his possession a certain amount of property which he can spare, and that there are but two other men in existence, B and C. Suppose, further, that A loves his two fellow-men equally, but that B is in great want, while C is in affluence. Will not the love of A lead him to put the property at his disposal in the hands of B? But suppose, again, that A owes to C the exact amount of the property in question, and has no other means of paying him, while C by his own labor in past time produced the value which A now possesses and has promised to repay. Love may still prompt the latter to give the property to his suffering brother B, but the law of right interposes an absolute veto, and requires him to put it in the hands of C. *Suum cuique.* There is no alternative, the voice of conscience is imperative and clear. Hence the moral law recognizes a principle of right, distinct from love; it requires justice before generosity. And as love is not the only moral virtue in man, so it is not the only moral perfection in God. The Most High is just, as well as benevolent; and therefore he cannot treat sin as merely a disease to be cured, or a misfortune to be pitied, but rather as a wrong to be punished. To illustrate this point still further, we will suppose but one created being in the universe, and that being to commit sin. What must be God's feeling and attitude towards him in view of the sin? Plainly there will be in God a sentiment of displeasure with him for the sin as such, whether this displeasure will benefit the sinner or not. God must condemn the wrong; he cannot be supposed to look upon sin as he would upon mere calamity. Even Dr. Bushnell admits this; for he says: "There is a wrath-principle in God, — a wrath-impulse, which puts him down upon wrong." But he represents this wrath-principle as blind and without any strictly moral quality. It is under the absolute sway of love. But such a view is not in harmony with the biblical account of God. In him, the Perfect One, there is no impulse which is too strong against sin, no impulse against wrong, as wrong, which must be ruled and repressed by reason. In a being absolutely perfect, impulse and reason are at one. In a holy God the wrath-impulse is holy, and he cannot be satisfied without a proper expression of it. For not only does this principle tend by its own nature to express itself, but an expression of it is requisite in order to a knowledge of God's true character on the part of his intelligent offspring; and therefore his holy self-respect and truthfulness would lead him to make it. We cannot, then, believe that he would on any consideration permit this evidence of what the sinner deserves to be unknown, that he would conceal his displeasure at sin, though the revelation of it must fill the sinner with anguish; for it would be hiding a fact of his own perfect nature and presenting himself to his moral subject in a false light. He will punish sin in fidelity to his own character, and because it ought to be punished. God cannot feel towards the evil as he does towards the good; he must show his disapprobation of sin as sin, and not simply as injurious, of sin as action performed, and not simply as a bad condition existing. Righteousness and love are not identical.

But is not the summary which Christ gave of the Mosaic law, making it all depend upon two things, love to God and love to man, incompatible with our view, and favorable to Dr. Bushnell's? It would be so, if Christ had used philosophical language. But he did not. His language was practical and popular, adapted to the moral state of man, and not to the claims of science. The great and only reason why perfect virtue does not exist among men is their want of supreme love to God, and of equal love to one another. Let selfishness give place to love, and human nature would be restored to a perfect state. The voice of conscience would then be heard in all the relations of life; for we only disobey the law of right when subject to the awful tyranny of selfishness. Let the equipoise of the affections be restored, and the claims of right will always be recognized as sacred and supreme. But the Word of God addresses itself to the actual condition of man. It enforces that claim of the eternal law of duty which, disregarded, leads to the disregard of every other, and which, obeyed, leads to the obedience of every other.

The law as revealed by Moses and summed up by Christ speaks only of man's duties to other beings; but he has also duties to himself, — to assert his own manhood, vindicate his own integrity, cultivate his own powers, bring his own nature to perfection, in a word, to love himself and seek his own good. This duty may be implied in the words of Christ, "Thou shalt love thy neighbor as thyself;" but why was it not distinctly expressed? Evidently because the Saviour was addressing himself to the actual condition of the race, — a condition in which there is no want of self-love, — and not setting forth the nature of right or wrong in the abstract, nor giving a scientific, exhaustive statement of what the eternal law of right demands.

We conclude, then, that Dr. Bushnell's idea of moral right, as expressed in this volume, is incorrect. Love is but a single form of righteousness; wrath against sin is another. But if his identification of love and righteousness is a mistake, his theory of the vicarious sacrifice is erroneous. The two go together; if one falls, so must the other.

III. GOD'S RELATION TO THE MORAL LAW.

The full title of Dr. Bushnell's work is this: "The Vicarious Sacrifice, grounded in Principles of Universal Obligation;" and the object of Part I.

is to show that there is "Nothing superlative in vicarious sacrifice, or above the universal principles of right and duty;" and the view which is foreshadowed by these expressions is boldly defended in the body of the work. A few sentences will verify this statement, and furnish suitable materials for criticism. "It is very obvious to any thoughtful person, that, in order of reason, whatever may be true as respects order of time, there was law before God's will, and before his instituting act, namely, that necessary, everlasting, ideal law of RIGHT, which simply to think is to be forever obliged by it." (255.) "The righteousness of God is the rightness of God, before the eternal, self-existent law of right." That righteousness "is by obedience to a law before God's will." (259.) "Such is right, and such is moral nature, as related thereto — both self-existent (sic) — that . . . were he to cast off right . . the crystal must so break, without regard to justice, by its own necessary law, and so he must irrecoverably fall." (243.) "Perhaps it is better not to say that he is *under* law, lest we associate some constraint or limitation, but that he is *in* it, has it for the spring of his character and counsel, and so of his beatitude forever." (308.) "What can we think or know of a goodness over and above all standards of good? We might as well talk of extensions beyond space, or truths beyond the true. Goodness, holy virtue, is the same in all worlds and beings, measured by the same universal standards; else it is nothing to us. Defect is sin; overplus is impossible. God himself is not any better than he *ought* to be, and the very essence and glory of his perfection is, that he is just as good as he ought to be." (57.) "Do we then assume that Christ, in his vicarious sacrifice, was under obligation to do and to suffer just what he did? Exactly this. Not that he was under obligations to another, but to himself." (58.) Finally, "It is the glory of our standards of goodness that they are able to *fashion, or construct, all that is included in the complete beauty of God.*" (Ib.)

This language is, to say the least, far too positive. Indeed, we have always supposed ourselves unable to find out the Almighty unto perfection, and have been wont to imagine that his moral excellence transcends our highest thoughts of virtue, as far as his omniscience transcends the knowledge we can compass, or his omnipotence the power we can understand. It has seemed to us impossible to think of him as merely a dilated man, — as being, even in kind, altogether such an one as ourselves. But the writer whom we are reviewing thinks otherwise. He claims to be a perfect copy *in minimo* of the Most High. By projecting the lines of his own moral being, he deems himself able to include within them the complete beauty of God. His words startle us by their audacity. The moral nature and government of Jehovah are in the grasp of his faculties, and he is competent to deal with them, without assistance from the Scriptures.[1] But let us look at his doctrine more closely, and see if it rests on a sure foundation.

In the first place, Dr. Bushnell teaches that "right, and the moral nature of God as related thereto, *are both self-existent.*" This, certainly, may be true, but it seems to us very doubtful. For if right and the moral nature of God are both self-existent, in any other sense than omniscience and the intelligent nature of God are both self-existent,— that is, if right is in any way independent of God, — then it follows that God is not supreme in the moral world; he is at best only an artificer,

[1] It will be recollected by the reader that Mr. Beecher, in "The Life of Jesus the Christ," uses language no less positive in respect to God and man as being of the same nature; as if men were literally and naturally sons of God, limited, indeed, for the present by reason of the flesh, but destined to enter hereafter upon a divine mode of existence. The language of many good men in this direction is perfectly amazing, and if it is not strictly pantheistic, it must be pronounced polytheistic: the Creator and the creature of the same genus! It is not well for Protestants who thus write and speak, to say much about the self-deification of the Pope. Yet we know the Christian zeal of these men too well to imagine that they feel in their hearts all which their words signify; and we doubt not the same charity should be felt towards not a few of the pretended successors of Peter.

not an original source; and there is something apart from him which is the ultimate object of reverence for every moral being. But such a view is established neither by conscience nor by reason. Conscience, it is true, pronounces the principles of right to be eternal and immutable; but so are the moral nature and judgment of God. It is as absurd to suppose a change in him as it is to suppose one in them. That which his mind approves as right we are made to look upon as right, and this is all that can truly be said. For reason affirms that the moral nature of man, as an effect, must be traced back to an adequate cause; it forbids us to postulate two causes when one of them is sufficient to account for the effect; and surely an Infinite Being is a sufficient cause for the moral nature of man.

Besides, the principles of right have their existence in moral beings only. Apart from such beings they no more exist than does sound without an ear, or light without an eye. As it is the eye which makes the vibrations of a certain ether to be light, and the ear which makes the vibrations of air to be sound; so it is the moral nature or conscience which makes the acts of certain beings to be right. The cunning of the weasel, the simplicity of the lamb, the fierceness of the tiger and the gentleness of the dove, are all alike good; but they have no moral quality, for these animals have not the faculty which creates this quality. The existence of right is therefore due to the existence of moral beings; it is the product of their spiritual nature, and that nature has its source in God. The ultimate standard of right is therefore the eternal judgment of God. This is all we can know; and this may be Dr. Bushnell's view, but his language seems to go further than this, and make the moral law more objective to him, and, as it were, independent of him, than we can admit.

In the second place, he applies the same standard of virtue to God and man, concluding from the fact that man can do no more good than he ought to do, or is under moral obligation to do, that the same is true of God. There can be no right action by him that is not required by the moral law. He would sin against himself, he would disobey the voice of his own conscience, if he were to do less for any being, good or bad, than he does. We cannot assent to this view of the case. It is doubtless a fair inference from Dr. Bushnell's theory, that righteousness and benevolence are commensurate and identical; but we reject that theory, and must therefore consider this view by itself.

Man is certainly bound to do all the good he can; but we are not sure that this is also true of

God. The Creator and the creature occupy different positions. If God is morally bound to do all the good he can, he was always bound to do this, and therefore an objective universe has always existed. Moreover, the number of beings and the grades of being have always been the one just as great and the other as high as they could be made without diminishing the aggregate welfare. Stones could not have been made trees, nor trees reptiles, nor reptiles quadrupeds, nor quadrupeds men, nor men angels, nor angels creatures of larger capacity. The scale could not have been raised nor depressed a hair's breadth. When God made the worlds, he exhausted the possibilities of right creative action for himself. Still further, if this theory be true, God is not a self-sufficing being; for his blessedness must be dependent on the perfection of his moral action, and that moral action is imperfect, nay, sinful, if he is not doing all the good he can *ad extra*.

Such a theory we cannot accept. It seems to us that there is a better view of God, which may be stated as follows: He was under no moral obligation whatever to exert his power in the creation of other beings. He would have been most blessed forever had he chosen not to do so. It was from no sense of duty, but from his own good pleasure, that he made the worlds. Our philosophy of creation is no philosophy at all, for we leave it where Paul left the great fact of election, in the supreme *eudokia* of the Creator. We also believe that he could have made the scale of created being higher or lower, without trampling on the law of right; and, in general, that it is purely optional with him either to put forth all his might, or to keep the greatness of it in reserve, a secret forever in his own bosom. We shrink from the hypothesis that the universe *fully* represents any of the perfections of the Supreme, that the Infinite One has put all his nature into expression in an aggregate, however large, of finite objects.

Again, with our view of the difference between righteousness and benevolence, — a view which is sustained by the language of every considerable people under heaven, and by the Sacred Record as well, — we can and do hold that God may love beings, once created, more than the moral law requires. That law commands us to love them according to their worth, God with all possible intensity, and men as we do ourselves. If this rule be applicable to the Infinite Maker, he is bound to love himself supremely, and all other beings in proportion to their natural and moral worth. But he sometimes does more than this. In the mystery of his sovereign good will he sets his affection upon some beyond the measure of their worth. Passing over the line of duty to himself and to them, he reveals a suprâ-legal goodness or grace. And such a goodness is not an absurdity; it is not like "extension beyond space," or "truth beyond the true;" for goodness is not the same as righteousness. It may be a degree of love, the want of which would be no sin; it may be a grace, transcending the claims of right. And such, according to the obvious meaning of the New Testament, is the grace of God in Christ to his own elect.

Dr. Bushnell does, indeed, make room in his system for a greater display of love to some moral beings than to others, yet only because the former can be benefited, while the latter cannot. He very properly concedes that God does not act in vain. Thus: "We are to see and make our due account of this one fact, that a good being is, by the supposition, ready, just according to his goodness, to act vicariously in behalf of any bad or miserable being, *whose condition he is able to restore.* For a good being is not simply one who gives bounties and favors, but one who is in the principle of love; and it is the nature of love, universally, to insert itself into the miseries and take upon its feeling the burdens of others. Love does not consider the ill-desert of the subject; he may even be a cruel and relentless enemy. It does not consider the expense of toil and sacrifice and suffering the intervention may cost. It stops at nothing *but the known impossibility of relief or benefit;* asks for nothing as inducement *but the opportunity of success.*" (42.) Applying this view, it appears that God has the same degree of love to all men, if not to all beings, whether friends or foes, holy or sinful; but his manifestation of that love, by suffering intervention in their behalf, depends on "the possibility of relief or benefit," on "the opportunity of success." Righteousness and love are commensurate, and therefore righteousness "does not consider the ill-desert of the subject;" that is a matter of perfect indifference; the only question is one of success. Love, or its equivalent, righteousness, will undertake no service which does not promise to benefit its object.

If this be so, one of the following propositions must be true, namely: (1.) The vicarious sufferings of Christ were borne by him without any reference to those who will finally perish; or (2.) his sufferings will somehow better the condition of the lost, instead of aggravating their guilt and woe; or (3.) he was ignorant of the future, and suffered in the hope of benefiting all, though that hope will be disappointed. If we accept Dr. Bushnell's view of the nature of the moral law, of God's relation to that law, and of the indispensable condition of action on his part in behalf of a sinful or miserable being, these appear to be the only possible alternatives. For he admits that some of our race will be finally lost; and this admitted, one of the propositions stated above must be true, if his doctrine is true, for a fourth hypothesis is inconceivable. But Dr. Bushnell does not teach that the vicarious sacrifice was limited, in the design of Christ, to the saved; neither does he teach that it will mitigate the woe of the finally lost; nor does he admit that Christ was ignorant of the ultimate results of his intervention. Every one of these propositions he denies, either expressly or by implication. But denying these, nothing remains but the abandonment of his whole system, so far as it is peculiar, or the acceptance of the doctrine of universal restoration. To this doctrine his reasoning gravitates irresistibly, and in this it will end with every consistent thinker.

Having examined the doctrine of "The Vicarious Sacrifice" as to the nature of the moral law and as to God's relation to that law, we proceed to notice what it teaches concerning

IV. THE PENALTY OF SIN.

This penalty is represented as being partly a natural consequence of sin and partly a remedial discipline.

Dr. Bushnell, it will be recollected, speaks of the moral law as "self-existent," along with God, as "before God's will" in the order of nature, and as "the spring of his character and conduct and beatitude forever." He is "*in* it," if not "*under* it;" yet truly under it, if all thought of restraint or of reluctant conformity be excluded. This, doubtless, is an error; the law is *in* him, rather than he in it; but Dr. Bushnell is self-consistent, for the most part, in carrying out his theory to its logical results, and therefore he speaks at length of "the law before government." On the supposition that any beings created under that law disregard it, he says: "As certainly as they are broken loose from right, they will be chafing in the bitter consciousness of wrong, doing wrong to each other, contriving wrong, writhing in the pains of wrong. Their whole internal state will be a nimbus of confusion. For though nothing is contrived in them and in the world to have retributive reaction, their simply being moral natures will compel them to suffer a tremendous shock of recoil." (241–2.) Mark also the following statement: "There is no express sanction to vindicate the law absolute, and no definitely understood sanction. Certain effects of disorder and pain would follow disobedience, but that they would follow *in any scale of desert*, we do not know. The justice which they will execute, therefore, is only a blind, *quasi* justice, if it be anything that deserves the name." (255.) Accordingly future punishment may not be anything which "deserves the name of justice," for "the fact of future punishment was in the law of natural retribution from the first, just as gravity was in the world before it was declared by science; for the penal disorders once begun are not reducible by us." (342.) Moreover Christ is represented "as only declaring that which lies in the simply natural causalities of retribution." (343.) Again: "The doctrine of endless punishment, taken as put into words, was never anything but a version of the fact, that retributive causes are naturally endless in their propagations."

But what of the law in government? It is only given to sinners and for their recovery to holiness; for this work says: "The instituted government and the redeeming sacrifice will begin at the same date and point, and work together for very nearly the same purpose. In the largest and most proper view, the instituted government will include redemption; for, *beginning at the point of transgression, already broken loose*, mere legislative and judicial action, plainly enough, cannot bring in the desired state of obedience." (244–5.) Note also the following language: "The instituted government of God is fast anchored in the terms of justice, declaring definite penalties." (255.) Yet "We shall very soon convince ourselves, it appears to me, that God has not undertaken to dispense justice by direct infliction, but by a law of natural consequence. *He has connected* thus, with our moral and physical nature, a law of reaction, by which any wrong of thought, feeling, disposition, or act, provokes a retribution *exactly fitted to it*, and, with qualifications already given, to the *desert* of it." (282.) Again: "In one view, all the statutes he enacts are explicatory, simply, of the law before government. In another view, they are only vindicatory of the same. So that the one fundamental principle of right contains, or demands, in a way of organic enforcement, all the statutes ordained; having these for its complete explication or fulfilment." (254.) Finally, "all the statutes we speak of are executory of this law (before government), else they are nothing." (250.)

A close study of these and other passages in "The Vicarious Sacrifice" will show that Dr. Bushnell teaches: (1.) That, properly speaking, God had no moral government over men before the fall. Both he and his moral creatures were *in* the eternal law of right, and a violation of that law by either of them would bring to the transgressor disorder and misery. This result may be called a sort of *quasi* justice, though not proportioned to guilt, nor in agreement with any scale of desert. — (2.) That, by reason of the fall, God was led to institute a government with "justice and penal sanctions." Yet these sanctions, appealing to fear and adjusted to the scale of desert, are inflicted by way of natural consequence. A law of reaction has been put into our moral and physical nature, by which any wrong provokes a retribution exactly fitted to it. — (3.) That this instituted government and justice have for their object the recovery of men to righteousness. They are parts of the redemptive plan. "The moral sense is mightily quickened by the arrival of justice, and the tremendous energy in which it comes." As "enforcing and sharpening moral conviction, the instituted law is a necessary co-factor in the matter of redemption." — (4.) That there is a "wrath-principle in God that puts him down upon wrong, and girds him in avenging majesty for the infliction of suffering upon wrong." Yet "this wrath-impulse is no law to God, requiring him to execute just what will exhaust the passion." It is no "fit conception of God's justice, that he will put evil upon a wrongdoer just because he is bad, and according to his badness, — that he will fly at evil-doing and make it feel just as much evil as it practises." God's indignation will be regulated by his wisdom, and the punishment which he inflicts will be graduated by what is necessary to secure the welfare of society. — (5.) That future punishment is not an infliction, and is not adjusted to desert; it was in the law of natural retribution from the first; for penal disorders propagate themselves. And therefore (6.) That the natural consequences of sin in this life are reformatory yet penal, and are adjusted, on the whole, to the guilt of men. This adjustment was not original, but was due to the fall of man; for it came with instituted government.

This is a brief account of the penalty of sin as described in "The Vicarious Sacrifice." In so far as this penalty depends on the moral nature of man, without respect to adjustments which are due to the fall, it is strictly a consequence of sin, is naturally eternal, and is wholly independent of God; for God could not have given to man a moral constitution that would not have ensured this kind of penalty. But in so far as it depends on the will of God and is proportioned to the ill-desert of man, it is exacted solely in the interest of redemption, and therefore ceases when the sinner is recovered to virtue, or has passed beyond the reach of hope. We are aware that Dr. Bushnell sometimes uses language which seems incompatible with this statement; yet we think our representation is not only in agreement with most of his language, but also with his idea of the moral law and the work of Christ. Hence the wrath-principle in God is only such a degree of force and sternness in the treatment of sin as will be best fitted to recover the sinner to good. The evil-doer is never made to suffer because he has done wrong, but only because, having done wrong and being in wrong, it is necessary for him to be made to suffer in order to be restored. Punishment is remedial. It is adjusted to the scale of ill-desert, not because it is retributive in design, but because it will thus be in the highest degree reformatory. The wrath of God burns, indeed, against sin in proportion to its malignity, but this wrath is a blind impulse which need not in any case be satisfied; it may be checked or overruled by wisdom or love.

Against this view of the penalty of sin we submit a few remarks. (1.) It is a purely speculative view, an inference from the postulate that righteousness and love are one and the same. As we have seen reason to reject the postulate, we see no less reason to reject the conclusion from it. But while the assumption that right and love are identical is the controlling one, it is not the only one required by Dr. Bushnell's view. For it renders many others necessary, in order to explain in any plausible way the statements of Scripture and the facts of experience. It compels us to assume the self-existence of a moral law, independent of God and superior to him; the creation of man as a moral being in that law, and subject to that law merely; the want of any penal sanction to that law, though certain evils, as a sort of *quasi* justice, naturally followed its violation; the institution of a moral government by God after the fall, recognizing degrees of guilt by grades of punishment; and the purely redemptive aim of this graded penalty. It is our belief that every one of these assumptions is necessary to the truth of Dr. Bushnell's theory, and that no one of them is supported by the general drift of biblical teaching. If they have any basis, it is furnished by the speculative reason only. (2.) It is incompatible with the testimony of conscience and of the Sacred Record. For conscience looks upon punishment as being, in its primary office and end, retributive, and retributive according to the scale of desert. It affirms that the bad, as such, ought not to be treated as well as the good, nor all the bad alike; but that penal evil should be proportioned to wickedness, because such a gradation is just and right, not simply because it is beneficial. This we hold to be the testimony of an unperverted conscience, the decision of a sound moral judgment. And it is sustained by the obvious sense of Scripture; for in many places the Bible represents God as taking vengeance on the wicked, and as punishing them according to the measure of their guilt. Moreover, this representation has respect very often to the eternal state, where he that knew his Master's will and did it not shall be beaten with many stripes. Besides, the Word of God distinctly teaches that men are not treated according to their deserts in this life. The wicked often flourish like the green bay tree, and have all that heart can wish; they live in honor and die in their nest; while the righteous often suffer want and shame, begging, like Lazarus, for a morsel of bread, and sinking at last, so far as this world is concerned, into unhonored graves. The evils of sin are not, therefore, in this life, proportioned to the ill-desert of men. They are rather, for the most part, admonitory, disciplinary, reformatory; but the balance will be restored hereafter. At the final day men will receive according to the deeds done through the body. The rich man who has his good things in this life, and is not led by the goodness of God to repentance, will then be in torment; while the poor man, who was chastened in spirit by affliction, and led to bewail and forsake his sins, will then enter into the joy of his Lord. In his theory, Dr. Bushnell has reversed the facts of the case. The eternal law of right demands punishment for sin in proportion to its malignity; but the economy of redemption arrests for a time the strict execution of penalty, adjusting the evils of sin to the purposes of recovery; but when the period of grace is closed, the last judgment will deliver up incorrigible offenders to the punishment of sin, according to the simple and perfect law of righteousness. Says Kant: "Reason represents to us the moral will as worthy of happiness. But we see that they do not coincide; nature does not effect such a meeting. There must, then, be somewhere a Power above nature, stronger than man, who will *uphold the moral order, will bring about the union between virtue and happiness, between guilt and misery;* and this being is God." It is no objection to this view that it has commanded the assent of the most thoughtful theologians and moralists since the advent of Christ.

We feel ourselves, therefore, constrained to reject the principles of religious philosophy taught by Dr. Bushnell, believing them to be erroneous and fruitful of error. These principles are three, namely, that the law of right is fully and exactly expressed by the law of love; that God is subject to this law in the same sense as are angels and men; and that punishment, so far as it depends on the will of God, is purely reformatory in its aim. It must be admitted that these principles agree with one another, and that, in the general drift of his argument, Dr. Bushnell is consistent with himself. More than this we are willing to concede,— every one of these principles has something in its favor. For if to love perfectly is not in strictness of speech to fulfil the whole law of right, it is to fulfil a great part of it and to ensure obedience to all the rest. If God is not bound by the moral law just as men are, that law is no less sacred and dear to him than to them. And if instituted punishment is not purely reformatory, the prospect and foretaste of it are often reformatory in the present life. The philosophy of "The Vicarious Sacrifice" is therefore partial, one-sided; for it recognizes only a moiety of the facts given by consciousness and revelation; but it is more than plausible, for it embraces large masses of truth, some of which have never before been exposed so fully to the light. Hence it is liable to be accepted as comprehending all the truth on the subject of which it treats. Hence, too, the difficulty of reviewing it justly, commending what is good, and rejecting what is evil. Perhaps it is wise, though it may seem ungracious, to point out the evil more carefully than if there were less of good mingled with it.

When a system of philosophy or religion professes to give the whole truth on a given subject, while it ignores or rejects a certain part of it, the system is, so far forth at least, a false one. And this falsehood is all the more dangerous because it is imbedded in truth.

"For a lie that is all a lie may be met and fought with outright;
But a lie that is part a truth is a harder matter to fight."

CHAPTER II.

INTERPRETATION OF THE LANGUAGE OF SCRIPTURE.

THE positive elements of Dr. Bushnell's system are many of them sound and good, but the negative are not; he affirms correctly, but denies incorrectly. Like the astronomer who stands on the earth and gazes at the moon, he has taken a mental position from which he can see but one side of the perfect sphere of truth. He readily perceives the manward aim of Christ's sacrifice, but does not catch a glimpse of its Godward aim. He sees the moral character and influence of that sacrifice, but is blind to its judicial character and value. Everything in his book looks to one end, the representation of Christ's death as expressive of compassionate love, and intended to awaken love in the hearts of men. Therefore, in his view, to justify a sinner by the blood of Christ, is to make him morally right by the persuasive power of the cross; to pardon him, is to release him from the control of inward depravity; to redeem him, is the same and nothing more; and to make propitiation for his sins, is to cleanse his heart from evil. Propitiation, justification, redemption, pardon, intercession, are therefore equivalent terms in the theology of this writer, all of them denoting the moral effect of the Gospel on the heart. We may therefore test the adequacy and correctness of his theory by ascertaining the ideas actually expressed by these terms in the Word of God.

I. USE OF THE TERM "VICARIOUS."

But we cannot enter upon this second and decisive part of our criticism, without protesting beforehand against Dr. Bushnell's use of the term "vicarious." And it seems to us that, in this respect, he may fairly be condemned out of his own mouth. For, after quoting a number of biblical phrases descriptive of Christ's death, he says: "The whole Gospel is a texture, thus, of vicarious conceptions, in which Christ is represented, in one way or another, as coming into our place, substituted in our stead, bearing our burdens, answering for us, and standing in a kind of suffering sponsorship for the race. . . Now the word *vicarious* is chosen to represent and gather up into itself all these varieties of expression. It is the same word, in the root, as the word *vice* in vicegerent, viceroy, vicar, vicar-general, vice-president, and the like. It is a word that carries always a face (?) of substitution, indicating that one person comes in place somehow of another. Thus a vice-president is one who is to act in certain contingencies as and for the president; a viceroy, for the king. The ecclesiastical vicar, too, was a vicar as being sent to act for the monastic body, whose duties were laid as a charge upon him; and the pope is called the vicar of Christ, in the same way, as being authorized to fill Christ's place. Any person acts vicariously, in this view, just so far as he comes in place of another. The commercial agent, the trustee, the attorney, are examples of vicarious action at common law." This is all quite correct, though it seems to promise very little for the peculiar theory of Dr. Bushnell. By what sleight of hand in the use of language, we involuntarily ask, is this word "vicarious" to take on a sense in harmony with the doctrine of the book? Let us see. Dr. Bushnell proceeds thus: "Then, if we speak of 'sacrifice,' any person acts in a way of 'vicarious sacrifice,' not when he burns upon an altar in some other's place, but when he makes loss for him, even as he would make loss for himself in the offering of a sacrifice for sin. The expression is a figure representing that the party making such sacrifice for another comes into burden, pain, weariness, or even to the yielding up of life for his sake. The word 'vicarious' does not say all, nor the word 'sacrifice,' but the two together make out the true figure of Christ and his Gospel." (39, 40.) By the aid of a "stile" Christian and Faithful passed readily over "the fence" and entered a "by-path" in a pleasant "meadow," a path which seemed to lead in the same direction as the one left, but which ended in darkness and Doubting Castle. By the aid of the word "sacrifice," skilfully handled, the author whom we are reviewing leads us into a way seemingly parallel to that in which we were just going with him, but which no longer "offends every strongest sentiment of our nature," and by a gradual trend is taking us to an opposite goal. He assumes in this passage two things: first, that the idea of "sacrifice" is that of personal loss, as, for example, the relinquishment of so much property in the animal sacrificed; and, secondly, that loss suffered for another is for that reason "vicarious." But does the Word of God speak of men as offering themselves in sacrifice, or rather as offering animals? Dr. Bushnell has employed the word in a modern and figurative sense, in order to shelter himself in an unauthorized use of the term "vicarious." Besides, loss suffered for another is not on that account vicarious, any more than a person who suffers for his king is on that account his viceroy, or a person who sympathizes with the president in a great domestic affliction is therefore the vice-president. Not one of the examples alleged by Dr. Bushnell justifies his use of the word in question. A little further on we are told, "that Christ, in what is called his vicarious sacrifice, simply engages, at the expense of great suffering and even of death itself, to bring us out of our sins themselves and so out of their penalties; being himself profoundly identified with us in our fallen state, and burdened in feeling with our evils." (41.) This language drops the idea of substitution, a "face" of which is always carried in the word vicarious. It represents Christ as suffering *with* the sinner, but not *in place of* the sinner. In every term adduced to explain the force of the root, *vice*, a proper substitution is expressed; but in this description of Christ's sacrifice the radical idea is omitted. Yet this description gives the author's view exactly. *Helpful sympathy in suffering* is what he means by vicarious sacrifice. But such sympathy is not, according to his own previous showing, vicarious; for it is suffering *with* the sinner and not *in his place*, not as his vicar, representative, sponsor, or substitute; and therefore Dr. Bushnell has misused an important theological term in the very title of his work. But it is not a biblical term; let us then see whether he has treated the language of Scripture any more fairly, for there are a number of terms, such as "intercession," "forgiveness," "propitiation," and "justification," which, as commonly understood, are inconsistent with his theory of the work of Christ.

II. INTERCESSION.

The sacred writers, it has always been supposed, looked upon the presence of Christ in heaven as a constant plea for the favor of God to believers, as an all-sufficient reason for the bestowal of grace upon the followers of Jesus; and they saw in the presence of Christ such a plea, it is also supposed, because he had offered himself a sacrifice for the sins of the people. But this view implies an influence of the Atonement on the mind and attitude of God towards believers, and therefore offends the judgment of Dr. Bushnell. Accordingly he writes: "Intercession means, literally, intervention, that is, a coming between; and it is not God that wants to be softened, or made better, for Christ himself is only the incarnate love and sacrificing patience of God; but the stress of the intercession is with us and in our hearts' feeling — all which we simply figure, objectively, when we conceive him as the priest that liveth ever to make intercession for us. We set him before God's altar, in a figure of eternal sponsorship, urging the suit of peace; though the peace he obtains by the suit of his sacrifice comes, in fact, from our mitigation, not from the mitigation of God." (71–2.) Can this be the meaning of the sacred record, when it speaks of Christ, or the Holy Spirit, as interceding for us? If the "eternal sponsorship" is but a "figure," can it be said to mean just the opposite of what it appears to mean? While it seems to bear the case of man before God, with a reason and plea for grace, does it, by this, aim really and solely to make an impression on the heart of man? If so, we must say with all reverence that a false idea is set forth for a good end; that the "altar-form" deceives the mind for the sake of softening the heart. And if such a method of doing good is right in the Most High, though wrong in us, it is greatly to be lamented that Dr. Bushnell has discovered the truth in this case, for a knowledge of the truth must sadly mar the power of the falsehood to benefit men. The Epistle to the Hebrews speaks of Christians as having "a great high priest, who has passed through the heavens, Jesus the Son of God," a "forerunner who for us is entered into that within the veil," who hath an "unchangeable priesthood," and is therefore "able to save to the uttermost all that come unto God by him, seeing he ever liveth to make intercession for them," and who "is entered into heaven itself, now to appear in the presence of God for us." Similar language is found in the Epistle to the Romans: "Who is he that condemneth? It is Christ that died, yea, rather, that is risen again, who is even at the right hand of God, who also maketh intercession for us." The "intervention," it will be observed, is in heaven, and is in behalf of those who believe. Both these circumstances agree with the common view; the place suggests influence on the mind or attitude of God rather than on the minds of men; and the preposition "for," or "in behalf of," accords with that view, rather than with the theory of direct influence on the hearts of Christians. The same verb is used in a few other places. Writing to the Christians in Rome, Paul declares that "the Spirit itself," that is, the Holy Spirit, "maketh intercession for us with groanings which cannot be uttered," and likewise that this same Spirit "maketh intercession for the saints according to the will of God." Reference is made in both these expressions to the aid which the Divine Spirit affords to Christians when they come before God in prayer for his blessing. Once more in the same epistle we find the word in question: "Wot ye not what the Scripture saith of Elias? how he maketh intercession to God against Israel," etc., that is, the term is used to signify a plea addressed to God against a sinful people; and it appears to have about the same sense in the report of Festus to Agrippa and his court concerning Paul: "Ye see this man, about whom all the multitude of the Jews have dealt with me," or made intercession with me. These are all the passages in the New Testament which contain the term in question, and in every one of them it signifies to appear before God, or a human ruler, with some reason or plea, in favor or against another party. It never denotes an intervention or effort in behalf of God, or the ruler, to change the moral attitude of the sinful subject. Josephus makes use of the word in a single instance, saying, "Lucius Lentulus, the consul, freed the Jews that are in Asia from service in the army, at my intercession for them" (Ault. xiv. x. 13); and its meaning is precisely the same as in the New Testament. It is also worthy of note as making against the exposition of Dr. Bushnell, that neither Christ nor the Holy Spirit is ever said in the New Testament to intercede for unbelievers. It is only for believers, for those who love God and seek his favor, that the Saviour appears as a sponsor or advocate in heaven. In conclusion, we are required to say that Dr. Bushnell has interpreted this important term without any proper regard to its actual meaning and use, and by so doing has saved his theory at too great a sacrifice; for a theory which can only be saved by perverting the sense of God's Word costs more than it is worth.

III. FORGIVENESS.

Why is an unexampled meaning given to this word by Dr. Bushnell? The question need not be answered; but of this we are certain, that the principles of his religious philosophy demand this unexampled meaning. For if righteousness is nothing but love, then penalty is but a means of reformation; and if reformation is once effected, nothing more is to be done, punishment has no office to perform, and falls away of course. But if there is need of pardon after repentance, penalty must be retributive as well as restorative, and righteousness is not one and the same with benevolence. Let us, then, look at a few sentences of his work: "The very light notions prevalent concerning remission, or forgiveness, . . . make it necessary to revise our impressions at this point." And, having noticed briefly the prevalent notions, he goes on thus: "What, then, is remission, more sufficiently conceived? The word, both in Greek and English, is a popular word, which signifies, in common speech, a *letting go;* that is, a letting go of blame. . . But though God accommodates our understanding, in the use of this rather superficial word, we can easily see, that his relations to a sinning soul under his government, taken hold of, as it is, already, by the retributive causes arrayed in nature itself for the punishment of transgression, are so different from those of a man to a wrong-doing fellow-man, that a mere letting go, or consenting no longer to blame, really accomplishes nothing as regards the practical release of sin. . . *We ought to be sure beforehand*, that the Scripture will not leave the matter here, but will somehow manage to strike a deeper key. And we find, as we go into the inquiry, that we have, at least, three distinct forms of expression given us, to accommodate our uses. . . Thus, if we are thinking of God's displeasure, we have the word 'remission,' that speaks of releasing the blame; and we often use the much deeper word, 'forgiveness,' in the same superficial sense. . . If, again, we think of our sin as *a state of moral incapacity and corruption*, fastened upon us by the retributive causes which our sin has provoked, we are allowed to speak of 'forgiveness' as the 'taking away' of our sin; just as we may of being 'healed,' 'washed,' 'reconciled,' 'delivered,' 'turned away,' 'made free.' Here we conceive that God is able, in the declaration of his righteousness, to get such a hold of the souls sweltering in disorder, under the natural effects of transgression, as to bring them out of their disorder into righteousness. . . They receive the executed fact of remission, or spiritual release. Otherwise, under a mere letting go, the bad causes hold fast like fire in brimstone, refusing to be cheated of their prey. The same is true of forgiveness." (423, seq.)

On these sentences it may be remarked: (1.) That they comprise the substance of the writer's argument for setting aside the common idea of forgiveness as insufficient for the purposes of theology;[1] (2.) That they reveal the state of mind in which he is ready to interpret the word of God, — "We ought to be sure beforehand, that the Scriptures will somehow manage to strike a deeper key;"[2] (3.) That they betray an astonishing levity in speaking of God's displeasure at sin; —

[1] Dr. Bushnell does not attempt to show that the meaning which he gives to "remission" and "forgiveness" is required by the context in any passage of the New Testament where one of these words is used. He does not even seem to have inquired whether other and deeper terms are not employed, along with pardon or remission, making the common, "superficial" sense of these the only tenable one, the only one that will save the writers from the charge of tautology.

[2] This "being sure beforehand" is one of the worst states of mind in which to study the Scriptures on a doubtful point. To make sure of a religious theory beforehand, on philosophical grounds, and then come to the Sacred Record for confirmation, is, to say the least, unwise, especially if that theory contradicts the obvious or *prima facie* sense of passages in that Record; for the chances are that the mind will set aside the true meaning of the inspired Word, and interpret its own theory into that Word.

God's letting go his displeasure, consenting no longer to blame, is a very light matter indeed, and a term which signifies only that has but a superficial sense; (4.) That they suggest a very careless use of the New Testament; for the words "remission" and "forgiveness" commonly represent the same Greek term, *aphesis;* (5.) That they prove him to understand by forgiveness of sin the "taking away" of our sin, regarded as a "state of moral incapacity and corruption;" and (6.) That all these positions may be traced to the writer's view of instituted penalty as their proximate source, and to his view of the nature of moral law as their original source. Instituted penalty is a light matter with him; or, rather, it is a great good; to remit it would be an injury rather than a blessing. The removal of the natural effects of sin is the only thing which has a look of importance to him, — or *can* have such a look.

The word *aphesis* occurs seventeen times in the New Testament, and fourteen times it is followed by the word "sins," or an equivalent term. Eight times it is translated in the common version "remission," and six times "forgiveness." In one other instance, "Without shedding of blood there is no remission," "of sins" is doubtless to be supplied to complete the sense. It may be well to transcribe these passages for the reader's convenience. "This is my blood of the New Covenant which is shed for many, for the remission of sins;" "The baptism of repentance, for the remission of sins;" "He that shall blaspheme against the Holy Ghost hath never forgiveness;" "To give knowledge of salvation unto his people in remission of their sins;" "Preaching the baptism of repentance for the remission of sins;" "That repentance and remission of sins should be preached in his name;" "Repent and be baptized, every one of you, in the name of Jesus Christ, for remission of sins;" "To give repentance to Israel and remission of sins;" "Through his name every one who believes in him shall receive remission of sin;" "Through this man forgiveness of sins is preached to you;" "To open their eyes, that they may turn from darkness to light, and from the power of Satan to God, that they may obtain forgiveness of sins;" "In whom we have redemption through his blood, the forgiveness of sins;" "but where there is remission of these"—the sins just mentioned—"there is no longer offering for sin."[1]

Even a cursory reading of these passages is enough to make it evident that no one of them requires us to give any but the usual meaning to the words "remission" and "forgiveness." For

[1] Matt. xxvi. 28; Mark i. 4; iii. 29; Luke i. 77; iii. 3; xxiv. 47; Acts ii. 38; v. 31; x. 43; xiii. 38; xxvi. 18; Eph. i. 7; Col. i. 14; Heb. x. 18.

they speak of "righteousness," "faith," "turning from darkness to light, from the power of Satan to God," and even of baptism, which is the prescribed sign of "repentance," as antecedent in the order of nature, and, indeed, prerequisite to the "forgiveness of sins." But according to Dr. Bushnell's theory of the divine act signified by the forgiveness of sins, it is incredible that this act should be set forth as a consequence of repentance and faith, nay, more, as an end to be secured by them; for if, as he avers, forgiveness is the act of "taking away our sin, regarded as a state of moral incapacity and corruption," it cannot differ from the divine act of working repentance or faith in the soul. For how can "the moral incapacity and corruption" of the spirit be more effectually removed than by a radical change of mind, expressing itself in faith and love? The objection which we now urge is fatal to this novel interpretation of the word *aphesis*, represented in our version by "remission" and "forgiveness."

We have looked at all the places in which the *noun* appears, and it may now be well to glance at a few in which the corresponding verb is employed. The Saviour taught his disciples to pray, "Forgive us our debts, as we forgive our debtors," and then remarked, "If ye forgive men their trespasses, your heavenly Father will also forgive you."

(Matt. vi. 12, 14.) With this language should be compared the Saviour's language in Matt. xviii. 23, sq.: "The lord of that servant, moved with compassion, released him, and forgave him the debt;" and verse 27: "Then having called him, his lord saith unto him, Thou wicked servant, I forgave thee all that debt, because thou besoughtest me," etc. These passages teach clearly enough, (1.) That divine forgiveness, as represented by this verb, is not a work of grace in the hearts of men. It may presuppose such a work, and be conditioned on it, but it cannot be identical with it. (2.) That "forgiveness" is the same act in kind, whether performed by God or by man. This is evident from both the passages cited. It is hardly necessary for us to bring forward other texts; for Dr. Bushnell disdains such humble methods of ascertaining the meaning and use of words.

Yet we must notice briefly the word *charizomai*, which in several places is properly rendered "forgive." It is twice employed to express the remission of a debt. (Luke vii. 42, 43.) It is also used to describe in part the duty of the Corinthian church to the man who had been cut off from it for incest, but had repented of his sin: "Ye ought rather to forgive and console him, lest perhaps such a one should be swallowed up with overmuch sorrow." (2 Cor. ii. 7.) Again, in the same connection, we read: "To whom ye forgave anything, I also: for what I have forgiven, if I have forgiven anything, for your sakes I have done it in the person of Christ." (verse 10.) In another place, when speaking of his not being a charge to the Corinthian saints, he says: "Forgive me this wrong." (xii. 13.) To the Ephesians the same apostle writes: "Be ye kind to one another, tender-hearted, forgiving one another, as also God in Christ forgave you. (iv. 32.) To the Colossians: "And you also, being dead in your trespasses and the uncircumcision of your flesh, he made alive together with him, forgiving us all our trespasses." (ii. 13.) And once more: "Forbearing one another, and forgiving each other, even as Christ forgave you, so also ye." (iii. 13.) There is but one of these passages that would be likely to suggest to any careful interpreter Dr. Bushnell's view of forgiveness, namely, the words, "Whom he made alive together with him, forgiving us all our trespasses." But here the word "forgiving" need not be taken as explanatory of "made alive;" it may far better, especially in view of the plural object, "trespasses," be understood to denote an act contemporaneous with the "making alive," but logically dependent on it. It is therefore plain that the occasional use of the word *charizomai*, to give, in the sense to "forgive," affords no foundation for the extraordinary theory proposed in "The Vicarious Sacrifice."

Besides, it is worthy of note, that the sacred writers almost uniformly speak of the forgiveness of *sins*, not of sin. This phraseology can hardly be accidental. It must have been chosen because it expresses most exactly the thought which was in the minds of the writers. But the plural, "sins," does not suggest "a state of moral incapacity and corruption." Such a state might perhaps be called naturally *sin*, but not "sins," or "trespasses." Nor does the phrase, "forgiveness of sins," suggest the idea of making a person morally right in character; for man is a unit, and sanctification deals with him as such, works in the centre of his moral being by strengthening faith, hope, love, and thence outward, through volition, into all the details of Christian action. But "sins," conceived of as the ripe fruits of an evil nature, as the distinct violations of a just law, may naturally be mentioned in connection with forgiveness. For moral evil culminates in actions, and therefore retribution and pardon refer to actions; on the other hand depravity is a state of the soul, a preference of self to God; and therefore regeneration and sanctification have to do with sinfulness, or sin, with the root and not with the branches. They act by infusing into the root a new life, mightier through grace than the old, and thus reach the branches and the fruit. And so the regular use of the word "sins," as the object of "forgiveness," is incompatible with Dr. Bushnell's theory of what is meant by this term.

And, finally, it may be observed that Dr. Bushnell speaks of pardon, remission, forgiveness, as signifying in common speech a "letting go of *blame*," but never as a letting go of *punishment*, while the dictionaries give the latter a leading place in their definitions. Thus, Webster says that the word "pardon" is from *per* and *dono*, meaning properly to give back or away, and assigns it two meanings, namely, to forgive, and to remit as a penalty. He adds, that we pardon an offence when we remove it from the offender and consider him as not guilty; we pardon the offender when we release or absolve him from his liability to suffer punishment. Again, he assigns two meanings to the word "forgive," namely, to remit as an offence or debt, and to remit as a debt, fine, or penalty. And, lastly, he defines "remit" as signifying, among other things, to forgive, as to remit punishment, to pardon, as a fault or crime. All these words signify, therefore, a letting go of penalty, as well as a letting go of blame. But "The Vicarious Sacrifice" does not, we think, allude to the former sense, while it evidently belittles the latter. And the explanation is at hand: Dr. Bushnell's theory of the Divine Government determines for him beforehand what the words of Scripture must mean, and so what they do mean, — dictionaries and context to the contrary notwithstanding. This may be regarded as unduly severe; but the truth must be spoken with all the more emphasis when error has found an able champion.

IV. JUSTIFICATION.

The Greek word *dikaioun*, which is commonly translated in the New Testament to justify, was employed by the Seventy to represent forms of the Hebrew verb *tsadhak*, and the writer whom we are reviewing says that, after careful examination, he must reject altogether the alleged forensic or legal sense of the Hebrew word. He pronounces it a strictly moral term, and remarks (p. 411): "On the whole I do not know an example in the Old Testament where the original moral word referred to, whether translated righteousness, righteous, and be right, or justice, just, and justify, is used in any but a properly moral sense." Now it is singular, to say the least, that the studies of this gifted writer should have led him to a conclusion so different from the one reached in every age by the most eminent Hebrew scholars; for, turning to the lexicon of Gesenius, we find among the definitions of this word the following, — to have a just cause in a forensic sense, to gain one's cause, to pronounce righteous or just in a forensic sense, that is, to acquit, to absolve, and to justify one's self. Fürst, an authority hardly second to Gesenius, gives nearly the same definitions, thus, to declare righteous in judgment, to acquit or absolve, to justify or defend one's self. But these lexicographers may, of course, be wrong and Dr. Bushnell right. Let us, then, look at a few passages which bear on the point in question, and which are briefly noticed by him.

The first is Deut. xxv. 1: "If there be a controversy between men, and they come near to the judgment, that they may judge them, then they shall justify the righteous and condemn the guilty." Here the Hebrew verb, translated "they shall justify," expresses a judicial act. The judges are not, properly speaking, to pronounce a decision on the moral character of the parties, as related to the "law before government," but rather a judgment on their conduct as subjects of a revealed law. This fact could not have been made plainer by any form of speech. Indeed, the direction to the judges "to justify the righteous and condemn the guilty," implies their power to do the reverse of this, that is, justify the guilty and condemn the righteous. Nothing but a judicial sentence can therefore be referred to. And if the decision of a legal tribunal may be given by the original word here rendered "justify," this word does certainly express the idea of righteousness under "judicial analogies;" it sets forth one's relation to law and penalty; and is not therefore restricted to the purely moral uses allowed by Dr. Bushnell. Besides, we know that it is the function of earthly judges not to make character, to "righten" men inwardly, nor to pronounce character as a whole to be good or evil, but to declare men innocent or guilty, right or wrong, in some particular act or course of action; and the standard, to which they are bound to adjust their decision, is the civil law, a law which may or may not coincide exactly with moral right.

The second passage is Isaiah v. 22, 23: "Woe unto heroes in wine-drinking, and to men of strength in mingling strong drink, justifying the wicked for a bribe, and they take away the righteousness of the righteous from them." Knobel speaks of these verses as being a "woe against judges without conscience, who take bribes to be spent in drunkenness;" and Alexander remarks that "the effect here ascribed to drunkenness is not merely that of incapacitating judges for the discharge of their official functions, but that of tempting them to make a trade of justice, with a view to the indulgence of their appetites." Here, then, we have the word which Dr. Bushnell describes as "the original moral word," nowhere used "in any but a properly moral sense," chosen by the sacred writer to denote a strictly forensic act, and indeed an act by which a guilty person is pronounced righteous before the law, — *rectus in curia*. And the judges are represented as doing this for a bribe. The decision which they give does not express their real opinion; it is merely a legal sentence. It is also worthy of note, that they are said "to take away the righteousness of the righteous from them." Is righteousness in this case a moral quality? Can unscrupulous judges take away from any man his rectitude before the eternal law? They may pronounce him guilty of a crime against the civil law, when he is not, and may deprive him of his standing as a good citizen, by a judicial act; but they cannot touch his moral character. Dr. Bushnell must have submitted the language of this passage "to heavy practice," if we may borrow one of his phrases, before he found it in harmony with his view. Indeed, we regard the language of Isaiah in this place as illustrating that of Paul in Romans i. 17, and elsewhere; for human judges are supposed, by the prophet, to give or take away righteousness, that is, to acquit or condemn by an official act, just as God is supposed, by the apostle, to do the same.

A third place in which the word under examination appears is Is. l. 8: "Near is my justifier; who will contend with me?" The verb translated "contend," in the last clause, denotes litigation, and we are therefore forced by the connection to say, that Dr. Bushnell's high moral word is made to do humble service, in the first clause, under "political analogies." Indeed, Dr. Alexander remarks on the participle which we have rendered "justifier," that "this is properly a forensic term, meaning to acquit or pronounce innocent, in case of accusation, and to right or do justice to, in case of civil controversy;" but his statement needs qualification; it goes about as far beyond the truth in one direction as Dr. Bushnell's does in the other. The word is frequently, but not uniformly, a forensic term. This is affirmed by all the best lexicographers, and their judgment is correct.

In Prov. xvii. 15, the same verb is used again of simply judicial action. "He that justifies the wicked, and he that condemns the righteous, even both of these are abomination to Jehovah." This proverb must refer to the action of civil rulers, and is analogous to Is. v. 22, 23, explained above. Equally certain is the use of the word in a legal sense, by Solomon, 1 Kings viii. 31, 32: "If any man trespass against his neighbor, and an oath be laid upon him to cause him to swear, and the oath come before thine altar in this house; then hear thou in heaven, and do and judge thy servants, to condemn the wicked, to bring his way upon his head, and to justify the righteous, to give him according to his righteousness." Here again we are deep in the judicial analogies; the wicked are to be condemned and punished, the righteous, justified and treated accordingly. The language has respect to civil affairs. The action solicited of God is retributive, not reformatory. On this point it would seem impossible for any one to entertain a doubt.

The passages now cited are sufficient to prove Dr. Bushnell mistaken in his view of the meaning and use of the Hebrew term in question. How he fell into so grave an error, it is not for us to say; but we may call attention to his remark, that "in three cases we find the expression, 'justify the wicked,' where the very point of the charge is that the wicked are taken into favor, passed as righteous, and so that moral distinctions, not forensic, are confounded." Now it is to be observed, that no one of these passages speaks of taking the wicked into favor; all of them speak clearly and only of making or pronouncing them righteous; and not of making them righteous by a change of character, — for this is not the function of earthly judges, nor indeed of any judge, acting as such, — but of pronouncing them righteous in a legal sense. In view of what law? Manifestly, of the civil law, or of the Jewish law, which was both civil and theocratic, though enforced by earthly magistrates. It is also to be observed, that all civil laws are presumed by those who make or administer them to be right. This was eminently true of those who had to do with executing justice according to the Mosaic law. Every transgression of it was a moral as well as a civil offence, — a sin against God as well as a sin against man. And a perception of the former aspect appears to have led Dr. Bushnell to deny the latter. But he does not attempt to explain how the righteousness of the righteous, this being understood in a moral sense, can be taken from them by wicked judges, nor does he prove by a breath of argument that anything except a judicial or forensic act is denoted by the verb in any one of the places examined. As the result of a pretty thorough study of the Old Testament, with the help of a Hebrew concordance, we affirm that the word in question is often used in a legal sense.

To complete the discussion, we now turn to the New Testament, and examine the use of the corresponding Greek term. In Matt. xii. 36, 37, we read as follows: "But I say unto you that every idle word that men shall speak, they shall give account thereof in the day of judgment; for from thy words thou shalt be justified, and from thy words thou shalt be condemned." In this verse the forensic use of the verb is just as certain as language could make it. The day of judgment, the account given, the source of justification on the one hand and of condemnation on the other, and the sentence itself, are all mentioned; so that we despair of finding any word which is used to mark a decision as judicial if the word translated "shall be justified" is not used for that purpose by our Saviour in the passage quoted. In Rom. ii. 12, 13, 16, Paul writes thus: "For as many as sinned without law shall also perish without law, and as many as sinned with law shall be judged by law; for not the hearers of law are just before God, but the doers of law shall be justified . . . in the day when God shall judge the secrets of men by Jesus Christ, according to my Gospel." Here the apostle makes use of legal analogies, and the words "shall be justified" express a judicial decision. To deny this seems to us to be denying what is plainest in speech. Hardly less conclusive is the evidence contained in 1 Cor. iv. 4, when read with the context, thus: "But with me it is a very small thing that I should be judged by you or by man's day;[1] nay, neither do I judge myself For I am conscious to myself of nothing; yet not in this am I justified, but he that judgeth me is the Lord. So then judge not anything before the time, until the Lord come, who will bring to light the hidden things of darkness, and make manifest the counsels of the hearts; and then shall each one have the praise [due to him] from God." In this place the apostle declares that neither the judgment of his fellow-men, nor that of his own conscience, is authoritative and perfect. As a steward of the mysteries of God he was acquitted by his own conscience of having been unfaithful to the Corinthians; but this acquittal was not final; for the Lord alone is judge, and only at his coming did the apostle expect to hear the infallible decision. It seems to us, then, that the forensic sense of the term "justified" is unquestionable in this passage. The same is true of it, likewise, in Rom. viii. 33: "Who shall lay anything to the charge of God's elect? God is he that justifieth: Who is he that condemneth?" Mention is here made of accusation, of justification, of condemnation, and no just interpreter can hesitate a moment in pronouncing the use of the word forensic. Yet it is applied to believers in Christ and is preceded by the words, "Whom he predestinated, them he also called; and whom he called, them he also justified; and whom

[1] In our version, "judgment."

he justified, them he also glorified." The word "called," in this place, refers to the divine act of regeneration, and the word "justified," to the judicial act by which a believer is absolved from guilt, and pronounced right before the law.

Besides the passages which have been cited and which may be said to demonstrate the forensic use of the Greek word translated "justify," etc., we may briefly advert to a few others. We are informed by Luke (x. 29) that a certain lawyer, who had tempted Christ, "wishing to justify himself," said to Jesus, "And who is my neighbor?" This he asked, not for the purpose of making himself right or just in reality, but for the purpose of vindicating himself against the charge of wrong, which, as his conscience whispered, was made against him by the words of Christ. Luke, therefore, employs the word "justify" in a sense derived from the forensic sense and closely allied to it. In another place (Luke xvi. 15) we read as follows: "Ye are they who justify themselves before men; but God knoweth your hearts." The Pharisees pronounced judgment on themselves, affirming that they were pre-eminently righteous, though God knew that they were miserable sinners. In still another place Christ says of the publican, "This man went down to his house justified rather than the other," and the meaning appears to be this, that his prayer was heard and his sins forgiven, — a judicial act on the part of God.

In Acts xiii. 38, 39, we read: "Be it therefore known unto you, men, brethren, that through this One the forgiveness of sins is announced to you, and that from all, from which you were not able by the law of Moses to be justified, in this One every one who believes is justified." Dr. Hackett, with the best commentators generally, regards "forgiveness of sins" in the former of these verses as substantially equivalent to being "justified" in the latter. But evidently forgiveness "rightens," not the character, but the legal state of him to whom it is granted. Again, Paul writes to the Romans as follows (iv. 6–8): "As also David speaks of the blessedness of the man to whom God imputes righteousness, without works: Blessed are they whose iniquities are forgiven, whose sins are covered; blessed is the man to whom the Lord does not impute sin." Here the phrases to "impute righteousness," to "forgive iniquity," to "cover sin," and "not to impute sin," are used as equivalent expressions, and all of them are judicial instead of moral. God is a gracious ruler who accepts union with Christ by faith as a substitute for perfect and personal obedience to the law. Hence the penalty of sin is remitted and the believer is looked upon as right before the law, that is, as no longer exposed to the penalty which it threatens.

It has now been sufficiently proved that Dr. Bushnell's attempt to set aside the use of δικαιοῦν, as a judicial term, is an utter failure. The word has the meaning commonly assigned to it by evangelical scholars, and is wholly incompatible with his view of salvation through Christ. For if God is one "who justifieth the ungodly," and if we are "justified in the blood of Christ" (Romans iv. 5; v. 9), that is, have in his blood the proper reason for our justification, as Paul expressly states, it follows that our moral state or conduct is not that in consideration of which we are accepted as just, but rather the sacrificial death of Christ. His atonement, therefore, has a Godward as well as a manward efficacy.

V. PROPITIATION.

This word occurs in the crucial passage (Rom. iii. 25, 26): "Whom God set forth as a propitiation, through faith, in his blood, for the exhibition of his righteousness, because of the passing by of the sins formerly committed, in the forbearance of God; for the exhibition of his righteousness in this present time, that he may be just and the justifier of him who believes in Jesus."

The meaning of the sacred writers in any place must be ascertained by a careful study of the words which they use, in the light of the context. It has often been shown that the verb "propitiate" may always be presumed to have for its direct object a superior being who is offended. Of course the noun "propitiation" has respect also to such an object. This noun occurs but three times in the common version of the New Testament, and it will be interesting, therefore, to look at the passages. John writes thus in his first epistle: "If any one have sinned, we have an advocate with the Father, Jesus Christ, the righteous. And he is a propitiation for our sins, and not for ours only, but also for the whole world."[1] Now it is plain, for several reasons, that the term "propitiation" must, in this place, be supposed to have God for its object. (1.) Jesus Christ is here called a paraclete or advocate, while in the Gospel of John this title is given to the Holy Spirit; and the twofold application of the term is best accounted for by assuming that the Holy Spirit presents Christ and his work to men, while Jesus Christ himself, by his presence above, presents the same to God; the Spirit pleading with the people in behalf of God, and the Redeemer pleading with God in behalf of the people. (2.) The expression, "*with* the

[1] 1 John ii. 1, 2.

Father," — πρὸς τὸν πατέρα, — denotes in the original some sort of motion, tendency, or effort towards the Father, showing that, in this case, the plea is addressed to him. (3.) John speaks of the "propitiation" as having respect to "sins," — not to a bad state of heart, or to renovation of character, but to "sins" already committed. How this can be deemed a natural expression of the view taught by "The Vicarious Sacrifice" is not easy to see. And (4.) The "propitiation" represented by the presence of Christ is said to be, not for the sins of believers only, but also for the whole world. Does the moral power of Christ's sacrifice reach all the world of mankind and turn them back to God? Can it even be said to have reached all those who were saved before the advent of Christ? If not, then, according to the doctrine of "The Vicarious Sacrifice," the death of Christ has no bearing on the rescue of multitudes who will be found in heaven at last; for it has only a manward efficacy, with no retrospective influence on the salvation of patriarchs or prophets.

In the same epistle John writes, "In this is love, not that we loved God, but that he loved us, and sent his Son a propitiation for our sins."[1] It has been thought unaccountable that God, out of love to men, should send his Son to turn away his own

[1] 1 John iv. 10.

wrath from them, by suffering for their sins. But love and wrath are compatible, homogeneous affections. Men may be objects of God's care, solicitude, and love in view of their high powers and natural worth, but objects of his just displeasure in view of their moral conduct. It is not, therefore, surprising that he should be unwilling to show mercy to them, except in such a way as comports with righteousness. His displeasure with their sins is just as holy and inviolable as his love to their God-given nature; and therefore love to them leads him to satisfy his righteous indignation at sin, in order that he may pour out his grace on the sinful. And so he propitiates himself, or his own moral nature, by suffering in the person of his Son the penalty due to them for their sins. It is indeed a costly sacrifice, and it reveals a wondrous love to men. In this is love, that he sent his Son to be a propitiation for our sins.

Lastly, in the Epistle to the Romans Paul writes thus: "Whom God set forth a propitiation in his blood."[1] The Greek word in this passage is from the same root as the noun employed by John, but it is properly an adjective used as a noun, and denoting, literally, the lid of the ark, on which the blood of a sin-offering was most solemnly sprinkled, by the high priest, on the great day of Atonement.

[1] Romans iii. 25.

That lid, with the blood upon it, represented the highest idea of propitiation under the Mosaic economy, and was therefore used as a metaphor in describing Christ crucified for the sins of the people. God looked upon the cover of the ark sprinkled with blood, and his just indignation was turned away from Israel, full scope was given to his love and clemency, and so he was said to be made propitious. In like manner, having in his love to men honored his righteousness by the sacrifice of Christ, he looks upon the Saviour in his blood as a sufficient ground or reason for showing mercy to sinners, and can be just while justifying all who believe. In this passage, therefore, it is God who is propitiated, and not the ungodly. Righteousness is honored, that love may have free course.

The Greek verb, from which the two words translated propitiation are derived, is found in two passages of the New Testament. The first is the prayer of the publican, "God, be merciful to me, a sinner;" where the term is used with reference to God, to denote the result of propitiation in his mind and action; and we suppose it would be equally correct to translate the prayer, "O God, be propitiated towards me, a sinner," the suppliant having in mind the temple sacrifices as the appointed means of turning away the wrath of God from a penitent sinner. The other is the language of the Epistle to the Hebrews: "Whence it behoved him to be made in all respects like his brethren, that he might be a merciful and faithful high priest in things pertaining to God, to propitiate for the sins of the people." Something must here be understood, for it would be absurd to speak of propitiating the sins of the people, — ἱλάσκεσθαι τὰς ἁμαρτίας τοῦ λαοῦ. Nor is it any improvement to supply the word people, or men; the only word to be thought of is God: "To propitiate God for the sins of the people." So Winer, Meyer, Kurtz, Philippi, Smeaton, and many others.

That the word often denotes a change in the attitude of God to sinners is evident from its use in the Septuagint.[1] In the narrative of Jacob's preparation to meet Esau, his reason for sending before him drove after drove of cattle, sheep, and the like, is thus given: "I will appease him with the present that goeth before me;"[2] where the object certainly was to placate the offended chieftain. Again, it is written in the book of Proverbs that "The wrath of a king is as messengers of death; but a wise man will pacify it;"[3] where wrath is

[1] Though the verb is always compound, ἐξιλάσκομαι, in the LXX., yet, so far as can be discovered, with no difference in the meaning.

[2] Gen. xxxii. 20. An exact rendering of the words used by the LXX. would be, "I will propitiate his face," — a somewhat unsuccessful attempt to copy the Hebrew phrase, "I will cover his face."

[3] Prov. xvi. 14.

the object to be propitiated or placated, though the offended king is doubtless meant. Again, when the people had sinned grievously against God, in setting up a golden calf, and Moses, having destroyed it, was about to return into the mount, he said to them, "Ye have sinned a great sin; and now I will go up unto the Lord; peradventure I shall make an atonement for your sin;" that is, propitiate God and obtain pardon for your sin. He did not go up to produce a moral effect upon the nation, but to turn away from them the just displeasure of God, and secure the forgiveness of their sins. Equally plain is the reference to God in a remarkable passage of Numbers. The priesthood is promised by covenant to Phineas and his seed after him, "because he was zealous for his God, and made an atonement for the children of Israel;" [1] for, by the summary justice which he executed upon two vile offenders, "the fierce anger of the Lord was turned away from Israel," and "the plague was stayed." The act which effected this was said to be a propitiation, or atonement, for the children of Israel. Besides the passages which have now been cited, the reader will do well to study the sixteenth chapter of Leviticus throughout, for the verb in question appears very often in that significant part of the ritual law. Nowhere in the

[1] Num. xxv. 13 (cf. verses 4 and 8).

chapter does it signify a moral influence upon men, by which they are made the loyal servants of God; everywhere it has for its immediate object the favor of God in the forgiveness of their sins.

But we turn to a very important statement in Lev. xvii. 11, quoted by Dr. Bushnell: "For the life of the flesh is in the blood, and I have given it to you upon the altar to atone (or propitiate) for your sins; for the blood atones by the life." According to this passage, atonement, or propitiation by sacrifice, was appointed by Jehovah; it was effected by an emblematical covering of the sin, or the object laden with sin; the covering was made by applying the blood of a slain animal; and the blood accomplished this by virtue of its being the seat of life, and so, when shed, the symbol of death. Propitiation was therefore made by death; for this was what the shed blood represented.

But Dr. Bushnell denies this. Having quoted the passage given by us, he adds: "Not that the life thus offered, the life made sacred and mysterious by such associations gathered to it, carries effect by ceasing to live, that is, by death symbolized in the sprinkling of it. No, it gets its effect as being life, the sacred, mystic, new-creating touch of life; for death is uncleanness itself, — no one touches a dead body without being made unclean, — but the blood is all-purifying; all things are by the law purged with blood." "Here, then, is the grand terminal of sacrifice; taken as a liturgy it is issued in a making clean; it purges, washes, sprinkles, purifies, sanctifies, carries away pollution, in that sense, absolves the guilty. The effect is to be lustral simply." (469.)

In this representation there is an element of truth, but it is not the whole truth. Purification is sometimes spoken of as the result of sacrifice; for an act of sin was conceived to leave behind it a moral stain which nothing but sacrificial blood could remove. Yet this is not the only representation. "Forgiveness" is also spoken of as the end of sacrifice. In the fourth chapter of Leviticus there is an account of the sin-offering and its result. When the whole congregation had sinned ignorantly, and it became known, a sacrifice was to be offered, "and the priest," we are told, "shall make an atonement for them, and it shall be forgiven them." Again, when a ruler had sinned ignorantly, and his sin came to his knowledge, he was to offer a sacrifice, "and the priest," it reads, "shall make an atonement for him, as concerning his sin, and it shall be forgiven him." The same words are repeated twice in speaking of the sin-offering which one of the common people was directed to make. A state of pardon was therefore contemplated as an end to be secured by sacrifices for sin. But neither this, nor purification, was, after all, "the grand terminal;" for the Bible nowhere represents his own justification or holiness as the highest good of man. That good is rather fellowship with God, while pardon and purity are conditions of that fellowship.

But in seeking to ascertain the meaning of sacrifice, we are not to look for the "grand terminal," but for the proximate end or effect. And this, according to the literal meaning of the Hebrew expression, commonly rendered to make atonement for sin, is a covering over of sin or guilt. To cover over the sin, or the sinner, is the technical phrase for expressing the proximate effect of sacrifice for sin. And surely there is nothing "lustral" in this. Yet Dr. Bushnell disposes of it thus: "The Hebrew word is *cover*, — the very same root from which our English word *cover* is derived. Thus, when we read so often, 'he shall make atonement for you,' 'scape-goat to make atonement,' and the like, it means the same thing as to make *sin-cover*, that is, reconciliation; the conception being, that sin is thereby covered up, hidden from sight or memory. Exactly the same thing is meant, when, using a different figure, it is said to be purged, cleansed, taken away." We ask for evidence that this last statement is true. But suppose it true; which of these is the ruling figure? Is it the one which is found in the technical, oft-recurring term, or the one which is found in a term occasionally used? If the former, then the sprinkled blood was not supposed to remove the stain of guilt, but to come between it and God as a cover, so that God might treat the sinner as if he were pure. If the latter, then the sprinkled blood was supposed to remove the stain of guilt; and how could the other figure be employed at all? If we start with the idea of a true spiritual cleansing, there is no room for that of covering. The fact, however, appears to be, that covering by the blood of sacrifice logically precedes pardon, purification, fellowship with God, or reconciliation. As we cannot infer from the use of "legal terms," in connection with bloody sacrifices, that the sole effect of the sacrifice of Christ was to put the believer in a new legal position; so we cannot infer from the use of "lustral terms," in the same connection, that its sole effect is to cleanse the hearts of men. If the fact that the application of sacrificial blood leads to pardon does not prove the former doctrine, the fact that its application leads to purity does not prove the latter. The death of Christ may well affect both the legal and the moral status of the same person; *and the fact that it affects his legal condition may be that which gives it power to affect his moral condition.*

But of what was the blood used in sacrifice an emblem? Dr. Bushnell says, "Of life, the sacred, mystic, new-creating touch of life." We cannot assent to his view. It seems to us very evident that he has entirely misapprehended the meaning of this symbol. For the bread and wine of the Lord's Supper represent the body and blood of Christ: "This is my body;" "This is my blood." But the apostle writes to the disciples of Corinth: "As oft as ye eat this bread, and drink this cup, ye show the Lord's *death*, till he come." Such a statement is conclusive. The blood of an animal offered in sacrifice testified of the death of that animal; the blood of Christ, the Lamb of God, represented him as slain, or crucified for us. It may be added, (1.) That shed blood is not the seat of life, for the life is no longer in it. It is suggestive, and therefore symbolical, not of life in possession, but of life lost, and the loss of life is death. (2.) That other parts of the slain animal were sometimes offered in sacrifice; yet no one has imagined that these *disjecta membra*, these portions of a broken body, represented "the mystic touch of life." (3.) That the slaying of the victim is often and formally prescribed. If the death itself was not significant, why was it made so prominent? When the law states what is to be done with the blood, and the flesh, and the bones, and the skin, and the entrails, it is surely needless to say that the animal must be slain, unless the death has meaning. It was in fact the great event of which the blood was a sign and a memorial.

"But death," we are triumphantly reminded, "is uncleanness itself; no one touches a dead body without being unclean." How does Dr. Bushnell know that "death is uncleanness itself"? The Bible nowhere speaks of it thus. Does he infer it from the circumstance that touching a dead body in certain cases made one unclean? He might as well infer that life is uncleanness itself, because generation and birth render those participant in them unclean. Does he infer it from the fact that death is the penalty of sin? It would be more logical to infer the opposite; for the law, with its penalty, is holy, being from God. Besides, Dr. Bushnell regards instituted penalty as reformatory in its aim and effect. The simple truth appears to be this, that God made choice of certain natural objects, which were commonly supposed to be unclean, or which he saw fit to have so regarded, as symbols of impurity. In this way the ritual law was made instructive to the people. Modern speculation has often sought for too deep a reason for this simple method of teaching moral truth, and for the selection of this or that object or act as unclean. Besides, it was not so much the state of death as the event of dying, that was suggested by the blood of sprinkling. The crimson stream, received from the expiring victim, spoke clearly of dying, and not of any subsequent state; and there is surely no more reason for saying that death in this sense is unclean, than there is for saying that birth is unclean. Indeed, the Word of God appears to afford no evidence at all of the truth of Dr. Bushnell's assertion, and we hesitate not to affirm the exact opposite. The blood, though a sign and emblem of the suffering of death by the vicarious lamb, was holy. It spoke of justice vindicated, of the law honored. In this light it was brought before God, who looked upon it and forgave the transgressor.

We return, therefore, to our position, that, as the bread and wine, representing the body and blood of Christ, show forth his death, and not his life, so the flesh and blood of the lamb offered in sacrifice for sin testified of the death of that lamb. And as the blood, the seat of life, was, when shed, the clearest sign of death, so was it used especially in covering the sin of the offerer from the judicial eye of God. This old view of the sin-offering is after all the best view. It is not brought from afar. It agrees with the chief terms employed and the ritual acts enjoined. For this kind of sacrifice was offered for *sin*. Moreover, it was named *sin;* not sin-offering, but *sin*. The blood, when sprinkled, was said to *cover over* sin, or the sinful soul. And before slaying his victim, the sinner laid his hands solemnly on its head, signifying the transfer of his guilt to the same. All these things are perfectly explained by the old view, and almost none of them by the new and lustral view. Hence we abide by the old and reject the new. The old is wine; the new is water.

Returning to the passage in the Epistle to the Romans, we say that the word "propitiation," taken with the words "in his blood," represents Christ crucified as a propitiatory sacrifice, — a sacrifice in consideration of which God is ready to show favor to all who make it their own by faith. Its proximate relation is, therefore, to the action of God, and not to that of man. Its direct purpose is to make it consistent with his righteousness for God to show favor to sinful man. The All Holy sees fit to vindicate his justice while approaching the guilty with terms of pardon. Hence the apostle makes the exhibition of God's righteousness the immediate object of the sacrificial death of Christ, though grace to sinners is the remoter object. Christ was set forth in his blood in order to exhibit the righteousness of God, and this exhibition was called for on two accounts: first, because God had not inflicted just punishment on all sinners before the coming of Christ; and, secondly, because he would not inflict such punishment on those who believe, from that time forward. For by "the sins formerly committed" must be understood the sins of men who lived before the advent of Christ. God had not at once inflicted the punishment which they had deserved, either upon the heathen in their blindness, or upon the Jews who had been guilty of spiritual sins for the pardon of which the Mosaic ritual made no provision. There is an allusion to the former in Acts xvii. 30: "The times of ignorance God therefore overlooked," and to the latter in Heb. ix. 15: "For this cause he is Mediator of a new covenant, in order that, death having taken place for the redemption of the transgressions under the first covenant, they who have been called may receive the promise of the eternal inheritance." Now it is difficult to see how the sacrifice of Christ could work any moral change in Jews or heathen who lived before his incarnation. If it could do this at all, it must do it in the state after death, not in the present life. But Dr. Bushnell says nothing of recovery from sin after death, and the Scriptures say nothing elsewhere of such recovery. We may, therefore, be sure that Paul does not refer in our passage to the moral influence of the cross, but rather to its judicial or rectoral influence. Such an influence might precede as well as follow the death of Christ; for God sees the end from the beginning, and to him Jesus was a Lamb slain from the foundation of the world. But the moral influence of Christ's character and suffering could have had no power on the hearts of men who were ignorant of him, and very little power over those who knew him merely by the light of Old Testament prophecy. It is unreasonable to suppose that Enoch, Abraham, or David, was led to faith in God by the view which was given to him of the piety, the love to God and to man, of the future Messiah. Not in this way did his name avail to save them. We reject Dr. Bushnell's interpretation, therefore, for this reason, among many, that it really puts all the generations before Christ out of relation to him and his cross. His name is not suffered by it to be the only name by which men can be saved. His vicarious sacrifice is the same in kind with that offered by any good man. It has no power with God, and its power with men is of course limited to those who have a knowledge of it.

But this is not all. If we assume, with Dr. Bushnell, that righteousness and love are in fact identical, the words of Paul are reduced to the expression of this thought, namely, God set forth Christ as a propitiatory sacrifice, in order to exhibit his love; and this exhibition he made because in his forbearance he had passed by the sins formerly committed. In other words: God would be self-consistent, and since he had omitted to punish sin in time past, he now shows his love by the death of Christ; the former is a good and sufficient reason for the latter. Is this the great conclusion in which the apostle's argument culminates? Can he find no better reason why God, who, according to this theory, is love and nothing but love, manifests his grace in Gethsemane, than the circumstance that in other days he had forborne to inflict prompt and condign punishment on men for their sins?

But we must not charge Dr. Bushnell with this impotent conclusion. He escapes it by giving up the plain sense of the apostle's language. Words are wax in his hands. For he defines *endeixis*, an *in-showing* or *effective impression* of; *paresis*, a *remission*, that is, a *removal* or *taking away;* and *dia*, with the accusative, simply *for*, denoting the end. So that the meaning may be thus expressed: God set forth Christ to impress effectually his holy love on the heart, for the purpose of taking away thereby the sins committed in past ages. But this, whether it be good sense or not, is by no means the import of the apostle's language. For interpreted by use, *endeixis* signifies *exhibition* or *manifestation;* *paresis* signifies *passing by*, or *omission*, not remission, and much less removal; and *dia*, with the accusative, means on *account of*, or *because of*. If, then, Dr. Bushnell is right in making righteousness and love identical, our statement of Paul's conclusion is correct; for he does affirm that God's forbearing to punish sins in past ages is the reason why he now removes those sins from the hearts of men, by impressing on the same his love. But we cannot suppose that any one will intentionally charge the apostle with so weak a thought in this cardinal point of his great letter.

It cannot be needful to pursue the examination further. For while it is evident that the theory of moral government defended in "The Vicarious Sacrifice" makes the entire work of the Father, Son, and Spirit, in redemption, to consist in renewing or "righting" the sinner's character, it is equally evident that the sacred writers did not so understand that work, and did not use the words intercession, forgiveness, justification, propitiation, as virtually synonymous with renewal, sanctification, and the like,—terms which are expressive of moral influence on the heart. "The Vicarious Sacrifice" emphasizes but a part of the redemptive work of Christ, while it treats with bitterness another part just as clearly taught in the Scriptures. And it illustrates more forcibly than any book we ever read, the marvellous power which a man of genius, under the influence of a theory, has to see his own view in all forms of speech, even in those which teach the exact opposite of it. Marvels of interpretation are set forth with a zeal and eloquence which charm the reader and make "the worse appear the better reason." And certainly it is a somewhat ungracious task to criticise the work of such a man. But there are times when it should be done and the claims of truth vindicated. In reviewing "The Vicarious Sacrifice" we have supposed ourselves performing such a task, pleading for the plain and certain meaning of Scripture, opposing a theory, most plausible, most captivating to the natural heart, but at the same time most incompatible with the teaching of Christ and the purest action of conscience. Let the reader "search the Scriptures daily," that he may "know the truth of these things," and be "nourished up in sound doctrine."

THE END.

MODERN LITERATURE

ON THE

PERSON AND WORK OF CHRIST.

This List of Works is not intended to be more than a selection from a great number of more or less importance.

NEANDER (A.) "The Life of Jesus Christ in its Historical Connection and Historical Development." New York, 1848.

LANGE (J. P.) "The Life of Christ."

DE PRESSENSE (E.) "Jesus Christ: His Life, Times and Work."

ELLICOTT (C. J.) "Historical Lectures on the Life of our Lord Jesus Christ, with Notes, Critical, Historical, and Explanatory." Boston, 1862.

ANDREWS (S. J.) "The Life of our Lord upon the Earth, considered in its Historical, Chronological, and Geographical Relations." 1862.

HANNA (W.) "The Life of Christ." 3 vols. New York, 1871.

YOUNG (J.) "The Christ of History."

ROW (C. A.) "The Jesus of the Evangelists."

BUSHNELL (H.) "The Character of Jesus; forbidding his possible classification with Men." 1861.

LIDDON (H. P.) "The Divinity of our Lord and Saviour Jesus Christ."

SCHAFF (P.) "The Person of Christ."

SEELEY (J. R.) "Ecce Homo: A Survey of the Life and Work of Jesus Christ."

RENAN (E.) "Life of Jesus."

PARKER (J.) "Ecce Deus: Essays on the Life and Doctrines of Jesus Christ."

PARSONS (T.) "Deus Homo; God-Man."

REUBELT (J. A.) "The Scripture Doctrine of the Person of Christ," etc. 1871.

ULLMANN (C.) "The Sinlessness of Jesus an Evidence for Christianity." 1858.

DORNER (J. A.) "The Sinless Perfection of Jesus," in the Am. Presb. and Theol. Review. 1863.

BODEMEYER (J.) "Die Lehre von der Kenosis."

MÜCKE (A.) "Die Dogmatik des XIX. Jahrhunderts," etc.

LIEBNER (T. A.) "Christologie oder die Christologische Einheit des Dogmatischen Systems." I.

THOMASIUS (G.) "Christí Person und Werk; Darstellung der Evangel. Lutherischen Dogmatik," II. 1–12.

PHILIPPI (F. A.) "Kirchliche Glaubenslehre." III. a, b.

BUSHNELL (H.) "The Vicarious Sacrifice grounded in Principles of Universal Obligation."

CAMPBELL (J. MCLEOD.) "The Nature of the Atonement and its Relation to Remission of Sins and Eternal Life."

YOUNG (J.) "The Life and the Light of Men." 1866.

BARNES (A.) "The Atonement in its Relations to Law and Moral Government."

ALEXANDER (A. A.) "The Atonement."

SMEATON (G.) "The Doctrine of the Atonement as taught by Christ himself."

SMEATON (G.) "The Doctrine of the Atonement as taught by the Apostles."

WALLACE (W.) "Representative Responsibility, a Law of the Divine Procedure in Providence and Redemption."

MARTIN (HUGH). "The Atonement in its Relations to the Covenant, the Priesthood, the Intercession of our Lord."

GARBETT (J.) "Christ as Prophet, Priest, and King."

SHEDD (W. G. T.) "The Atonement a Satisfaction to the Ethical Nature of God." Bib. Sac., Vol. XVI.

MARTINEAU (J.) "Studies of Christianity; Inconsistency of the Scheme of Vicarious Redemption, and Mediatorial Religion."

ELLIS (G. E.) "A Half-Century of the Unitarian Controversy," pp. 157–221.

SCHÖBERLEIN (L.) "Versöhnung," an Article in "Herzog's Real-Encyklopædie," etc. Bd. XVII.

EBRARD (J. H. A.) "Die Lehre des Stellvertretenden Opfer gegrundet in den keil. Schriften."

ÖHLER (G. F.) "Opfercultus des Alten Testaments," in Herzog's R. E.

WEBER (F.) "Vom Zorne Gottes."

KURTZ (J. H.) "The Sacrificial Worship of the Old Testament," in "Clark's Foreign Library."

RITSCHL (A.) "Die Neu-testamentlichen Aussagen über den Heilswerth des Todes Jesu, Jahrhücher für deutsche Theologie," VIII. 213 ff.

RIEHM (E.) "Über das Schuldopfer," Studien und Kritiken, 1854, I., 89 ff.

RINCK (W. F.) "Das Schuldopfer." Stu. u. Kr., 1855, 369 ff.

DALE (R. W.) "The Jewish Temple and the Christian Church," p. 186, sq.

OWEN (J.) "The Doctrine of Justification by Faith through the Imputation of the Righteousness of Christ."

PREUSS (E.) "Rechtfertigung des Sünders vor Gott."

LUTHER (M.) "Commentary on Galatians."

THOLUCK (F. A. D.) "Guido und Julius; or Sin and the Propitiator."

Valuable Works,

PUBLISHED BY

GOULD AND LINCOLN,

59 Washington Street, Boston.

GOD REVEALED IN NATURE AND IN CHRIST; including a Refutation of the Development Theory contained in the "Vestiges of the Natural History of Creation." By Rev. JAMES B. WALKER, author of "THE PHILOSOPHY OF THE PLAN OF SALVATION." 12mo, cloth, 1.50.

THE SUFFERING SAVIOUR; or, Meditations on the Last Days of Christ. By FRED. W. KRUMMACHER, D.D., author of "Elijah the Tishbite." 12mo, cloth, 1.75; cloth, gilt, 2.75; half calf, 3.50.

"The narrative is given with thrilling vividness and pathos and beauty. Marking, as we proceeded, several passages for quotation, we found them, in the end, so numerous that we must refer the reader to the work itself." — *News of the Churches (Scottish).*

THE TESTIMONY OF CHRIST TO CHRISTIANITY. By PETER BAYNE, M. A., author of "Christian Life," etc. 16mo, cloth, 90 cts.

☞ A work of great interest and power.

THE BENEFIT OF CHRIST'S DEATH; or, The Glorious Riches of God's Free Grace, which every True Believer receives by Jesus Christ and Him Crucified. Originally written in Italian by Aonio Paleario, and now Reprinted from an Ancient English Translation. With an Introduction by Rev. JOHN AYER, M. A. 16mo, cloth, 75 cts.

WREATH AROUND THE CROSS; or, Scripture Truths Illustrated. By the Rev. A. MORTON BROWN, D. D. Recommendatory Preface, by JOHN ANGELL JAMES. With a beautiful Frontispiece. 16mo, cloth, 1.00.

EXTENT OF THE ATONEMENT IN ITS RELATION TO GOD AND THE UNIVERSE. By Rev. THOMAS W. JENKYN, D.D., late President of Coward College, London. 12mo, cloth, 1.50

We consider this volume as setting the long and fiercely agitated question, as to the extent of the Atonement, completely at rest. Posterity will thank the author, till the latest ages, for his illustrious argument." — *N. Y. Evangelist.*

CHRIST IN HISTORY. By ROBERT TURNBULL, D. D. A New and Enlarged Edition. 12mo, cloth, 1.75.

THE SCHOOL OF CHRIST; or, Christianity Viewed in its Leading Aspects. Ry the Rev. A. R. L. FOOTE, author of "Incidents in the Life of our Saviour," etc. 16mo, cloth, 75 cts.

PHILOSOPHY OF THE PLAN OF SALVATION; a book for the Times. By an AMERICAN CITIZEN. With an Introductory Essay by CALVIN E. STOWE, D. D. ☞ New improved and enlarged edition. 12mo, cloth, 1.25.

THE PERSON AND WORK OF CHRIST. By ERNEST SARTORIUS, D. D., Konigsberg, Prussia. Translated by Rev. OAKMAN S. STEARNS, D. D. 18mo, cloth, 60 cts.

THE GREAT DAY OF ATONEMENT; or, Meditations and Prayers on the Last Twenty-four Hours of the Sufferings and Death of our Lord and Saviour Jesus Christ. Translated from the German of CHARLOTTE ELIZABETH NEBELIN. Edited by Mrs. COLIN MACKENZIE. Elegantly printed and bound. 16mo, cloth, 1.25; cloth, gilt, 2.00; Turkey mor., gilt, 3.50.

THE HEADSHIP OF CHRIST, and the Rights of the Christian People; A Collection of Personal Portraitures, Historical and Descriptive Sketches and Essays, with the Author's celebrated Letter to Lord Brougham. By HUGH MILLER. Edited, with a Preface, by PETER BAYNE, A. M. 12mo, cloth, 1.75.

THE MISSION OF THE COMFORTER; with copious Notes. By JULIUS CHARLES HARE. With the NOTES translated for the AMERICAN EDITION. 12mo, cloth, 1.75.

THE IMITATION OF CHRIST. By THOMAS A KEMPIS. With an Introductory Essay by THOMAS CHALMERS, D. D. Edited by HOWARD MALCOM, D D. A new edition, with a LIFE OF THOMAS A KEMPIS, by Dr. C. ULLMANN, author of "Reformers before the Reformation." 12mo, cloth, 1.25.

FINE EDITION, TINTED PAPER. Square 8vo, cloth, red edges, 2.25; cloth, gilt, 3.00; half calf, 4.00; full Turkey mor., 6.00.

The above may safely be pronounced the best Protestant editions extant of this celebrated work.

LESSONS AT THE CROSS; or, Spiritual Truths Familiarly Exhibited in their Relations to Christ. By SAMUEL HOPKINS, author of "The Puritans." With an Introduction by REV. GEORGE W. BLAGDEN, D. D. New edition. 16mo, cloth, 1.00.

THE BETTER LAND; or, The Believer's Journey and Future Home. By the Rev. A. C. THOMPSON. 12mo, cloth, 1.25; cloth, gilt, 1.75.

A most charming and instructive book for all now journeying to the "better land."

HEAVEN. By JAMES WILLIAM KIMBALL. With an elegant vignette title-page. 12mo, cloth, 1.25; cloth, gilt, 2.00; Turkey morocco, gilt, 3.25.

"The book is full of beautiful ideas, consoling hopes, and brilliant representations of human destiny, all presented in a chaste, pleasing, and very readable style." — *N. Y. Chronicle.*

THE STATE OF THE IMPENITENT DEAD. By ALVAH HOVEY D. D., Prof. of Christian Theology in Newton Theol. Inst. 16mo, cloth, 75 cts.

SAINTS' EVERLASTING REST. By RICHARD BAXTER. 16mo, cloth, 75 cts.

HARVEST AND THE REAPERS. Home Work for All, and how to do it. By Rev. HARVEY NEWCOMB. 16mo, cloth, 90 cts.

☞ The Pastor is often asked by his Sabbath School Teachers, "*What is the best Commentary on the whole Bible?*" You have here the answer.

THE PORTABLE COMMENTARY: A Commentary, Critical and Explanatory, on the Old and New Testaments. By REV. ROBERT JAMIESON, D.D., REV. A. R. FAUSSET, and REV. DAVID BROWN, D.D. In two vols. 12mo, cloth. $6.00.

Also, the same with the COMMENTARY on one page and the TEXT on the page *opposite*. In four vols. 16mo, cloth. $6.50.

This work will be found the most *compact*, as well as *reliable*, Commentary published, and is admirably adapted to the Family, Sabbath School Teacher, and all students of the Bible. Its theological opinions are Scriptural, its geographical researches are brought down to the latest periods, its explanations of God's Word are sensible and clear, and the whole forms one of the most convenient, useful, and really valuable Commentaries extant.

The work is in *two forms:* the PORTABLE, in *two volumes*, containing *only* the COMMENTARY; the other, in *four volumes*, containing *both* the TEXT and the COMMENTARY. The type is small, yet clear and distinct, and is furnished at a price so low as to place it within the means of all classes.

The work is commanding the general attention of Clergymen, Sabbath School Teachers, and all Bible students.

THE BREMEN LECTURES. On Fundamental Living Religious Questions. By a number of the ablest scholars of the day. Translated from the German by REV. D. HEAGLE. 12mo, cloth. $1.75.

DR. HOVEY, President of the Newton Theological Institution, in a prefatory note says: "I have given the Lectures a careful perusal; I am not surprised to find them rich in thought and admirable in style; indeed, singularly worthy of being put into the English language for the benefit of American readers; for they are noble defences of the Christian religion against fierce attacks from living adversaries; and, like all good defences of 'the faith once delivered to the saints,' they deal with central facts and principles, and possess a value quite independent of controversy."

CONTENTS OF THE WORK.

1.—*The Biblical Account of Creation and Natural Science.* By Otto Zöckler, D.D., Prof. at Greifswald. 2.—*Reason, Conscience, and Revelation.* By Rev. Hermann Cremer, Pastor at Ostonnen, near Soest. 3.—*Miracles.* By Rev. M. Fuchs, Pastor at Oppin, near Halle. 4.—*The Person of Jesus Christ.* By Chr. E. Luthardt, D.D., Prof. of Theology at Leipsic. 5.—*The Resurrection of Christ as a Soteriologico-Historical Fact.* By Gerhard Uhlhorn, D.D., First Preacher to the (late) Court of Hanover. 6.—*The Scriptural Doctrine of Atonement.* By W. F. Gess, D.D., Prof. at Gottingen. 7.—*The Authenticity of our Gospels.* By Constantine Tischendorf, D.D., Prof. of Theology at Leipsic. 8.—*The Idea of the Kingdom of God as Perfected, and Its Significancy for Historical Christianity.* By J. P. Lange, D.D., Prof. at Bonn. 9.—*Christianity and Culture.* By Rev. Julius Disselhof, Pastor and Inspector in Kaiserwerth.

LIFE AND LETTERS OF HUGH MILLER. By PETER BAYNE, Author of "The Christian Life." With a Likeness, a Bust, and Pictures of the Birthplace and the last Residence of Mr. Miller. 2 vols. 12mo, cloth. $4.00.

That Hugh Miller was, intellectually, one of the greatest men of his time, is a statement which no candid reader of these two volumes will question. Deemed a dunce by the schoolmasters of his boyhood, he rose from the humblest beginning to the highest position among the magnates of literature and science. The man or woman who begins this work will find themselves too deeply interested to stop until the end is reached. It is not only a deeply interesting, but a most instructive work, and should be read by everybody, old and young.

Gould and Lincoln's Recent Publications.

GOD WITH US; or, the Person and Work of Christ. With an Examination of "THE VICARIOUS SACRIFICE" of Dr. Bushnell. By ALVAH HOVEY, D.D., President of Newton Theological Institution. 12mo, cloth. $1.75.

This is a most able, thorough, instructive, and very timely work.

PROPHECY A PREPARATION FOR CHRIST. BAMPTON LECTURES. By R. PAYNE SMITH, D.D., Regius Professor of Divinity, and Canon of Christ Church, Oxford. 12mo, cloth. $1.75.

☞ A work of marked ability and of great interest.

DOGMATIC FAITH. An inquiry into the relation subsisting between Revelation and Dogma. BAMPTON LECTURES. By EDWARD GARBETT, M.A. 12mo, cloth. $2.25.

PROGRESS OF DOCTRINE IN THE NEW TESTAMENT; BAMPTON LECTURES. By T. D. BERNARD, Exeter College. 12mo, cloth. $1.50.

☞ A masterly production, and, as one distinguished Clergyman said of it, "It is worth its weight in gold."

THE JEWISH TEMPLE AND THE CHRISTIAN CHURCH. By R. W. DALE, M.A. On fine tinted paper. 12mo, cloth. $2.00.

"His work," says the *London Lit. World,* "is thoroughly able, and he proves himself to have complete mastery of the scholarship requisite for his purpose. He is eminently practical, but a vein of strong reasoning runs through the whole, and we feel that we are in converse with a masculine and sagacious intellect."

LECTURES ON SATAN. By THADDEUS MCRAE, Pastor of Presbyterian Church, McVeytown, Pa. 16mo, cloth. 90 cents.

The object of this work is to show the origin, character, and power of Satan; that he is not a myth as some are bold to assert, but a real character, as described in the Scriptures. The work is written in an interesting, vigorous style, presenting facts and arguments that must be convincing to every candid reader.

NOTES ON THE GOSPEL ACCORDING TO MATTHEW. Critical and Explanatory. Intended for Sabbath School Teachers, an Aid to Family Instruction, etc. By N. MARSHMAN WILLIAMS, D.D. With numerous illustrations. 12mo, cloth. $1.75.

The Notes by Dr. Williams have been approved, and highly commended by some of the ablest Ministers and Scholars of the denomination, and also by the press generally.

SEEDS AND SHEAVES; or, Words of Scripture, their History, and Fruits. By REV. A. C. THOMPSON, D.D., author of "The Better Land," "The Mercy Seat," "Lyra Cœlestis," etc. 12mo, cloth. $1.75.

A work unique, interesting, and instructive, giving illustrations of the use which God has made of particular passages of his Word. The biography of certain texts is more wonderful and more valuable than the biography of a hero.

PASTOR AND PREACHER; a Memorial of the late REV. BARON STOW, D.D. By ROLLIN H. NEALE, D.D., with an Appendix, containing extracts from a Memorial Discourse, by D. C. EDDY, D.D., and a Memorial Discourse by A. J. GORDON. Square 16mo, tinted paper, bevel boards, full gilt. $1.00.

A beautiful tribute to the memory of a good man; published in beautiful style.

Gould and Lincoln's Publications.

LYRA CŒLESTIS. HYMNS ON HEAVEN. Selected by A. C. THOMPSON, D. D., author of the "BETTER LAND." 12mo, cloth, red edges, 1.75.

FINE EDITION, TINTED PAPER. Square 8vo, cloth, red edges, 2.50; cloth, gilt, 3.50; half calf, 6.00; full Turkey mor., 8.00.

☞ A charming work, containing a collection of gems of poetry on Heaven.

GOTTHOLD'S EMBLEMS; or, Invisible Things Understood by Things that are Made. By CHRISTIAN SCRIVER, Minister of Magdeburg in 1671. Translated from the Twenty-eighth German Edition, by the Rev. ROBERT MENZIES. 8vo, cloth, 1.50.

FINE EDITION, TINTED PAPER. Square 8vo, cloth, 2.50; cloth, gilt, 3.50; half Turkey mor., 5.50; Turkey mor., 7.00.

THE EXCELLENT WOMAN, as Described in the Book of Proverbs. With an Introduction by Rev. W. B. SPRAGUE, D. D. Containing *twenty-four splendid Illustrations.* 12mo, cloth, 1.50.

FINE EDITION, TINTED PAPER. Square 8vo. New and greatly improved edition, cloth, red edges, 2.50; cloth, gilt, 3.50; half calf, 4.50; full Turkey mor., 7.00.

MOTHERS OF THE WISE AND GOOD. By JABEZ BURNS, D. D. 16mo, cloth, 1.25.

MY MOTHER; or, Recollections of Maternal Influence. By a New England Clergyman. With a beautiful Frontispiece. 12mo, cloth, 1.25; cloth, gilt, 1.50.

OUR LITTLE ONES IN HEAVEN. Edited by the Author of the "Aimwell Stories," etc. 18mo, cloth, 90 cts.; cloth, gilt, 1.25.

This little volume contains a choice collection of pieces, in verse and prose, on the death and future happiness of young children.

LITTLE MARY. An Illustration of the Power of Jesus to Save even the Youngest. With an Introduction by BARON STOW, D. D. 18mo, cloth, 40 cts.

GATHERED LILIES; or, Little Children in Heaven. By Rev. A. C. THOMPSON, Author of "The Better Land." 18mo, flexible cloth, 40 cts.; flexible cloth, gilt, 45 cts.; boards, full gilt, 60 cts.

SAFE HOME; or, the Last Days and Happy Death of Fanny Kenyon. With an Introduction by Prof. J. L. LINCOLN, of Brown University. 18mo, flexible cloth cover, gilt, 42 cts.

HEALTH; ITS FRIENDS AND ITS FOES. By R. D. MUSSEY, M. D., LL. D., &c., late Professor of Anatomy and Surgery at Dartmouth College, and of Surgery at the Medical College of Ohio. With Illustrations and a Portrait of the Author. 12mo, cloth, 1.50.

THE EVENING OF LIFE; or, Light and Comfort amidst the Shadows of Declining Years. By Rev. JEREMIAH CHAPLIN, D.D. A new, revised, and much enlarged edition. With elegant Frontispiece on Steel. 12mo, cloth, 1.50.

FINE EDITION, TINTED PAPER. Square 8vo, cloth, red edges, 2.50; cloth, gilt, 3.50.

RUTH: A SONG IN THE DESERT. 16mo, cloth, flexible covers, gilt, 60 cts.; cloth, boards, gilt, 65 cts. ☞ A neat and most charming little work.

THE CHRISTIAN LIFE, SOCIAL AND INDIVIDUAL. By PETER BAYNE, M. A. 12mo, cloth, 1.75; half calf, 3.50.

There is but one voice respecting this extraordinary book,—men of all denominations, in all quarters, agree in pronouncing it one of the most admirable works of the age.

THE CHRISTIAN'S DAILY TREASURY; a Religious Exercise for every Day in the Year. By Rev. E. TEMPLE. A new and improved edition, 12mo, cloth, 1.50.

☞ A work for every Christian. It is, indeed, a "Treasury" of good things.

THE CHURCH MEMBER'S GUIDE. By the Rev. JOHN A. JAMES. Edited by J. O. CHOULES, D. D. New Edition. With Introductory Essay, by Rev. HUBBARD WINSLOW. Cloth, 60 cts.

THE CHURCH IN EARNEST. By Rev. JOHN A. JAMES. 18mo, cloth, 75 cts.

CHRISTIAN PROGRESS. A Sequel to the Anxious Inquirer. By JOHN ANGELL JAMES. 18mo, cloth, 65 cts.

THE MEMORIAL HOUR; or, The Lord's Supper in its relation to Doctrine and Life. By JEREMIAH CHAPLIN, D. D., author of "Evening of Life," etc. 16mo, 1.25.

This is a precious volume, strictly devotional in its character, exhibiting the Lord's Supper in many aspects, presses home the lessons which it teaches, shows the feelings with which it should be regarded, and by its suggestions and admirable selections of hymns assists the communicant to prepare for this solemn service.

THE MEMORIAL NAME. Reply to BISHOP COLENSO. By ALEXANDER MACWHORTER. With an Introductory Letter by NATHANIEL W. TAYLOR, D. D., late Dwight Professor in Yale Theological Seminary. 16mo, 1.25.

THE MERCY SEAT; or, Thoughts on Prayer. By A. C. THOMPSON, D.D., Author of "Better Land," etc. 12mo, cloth, 1.50.

Fine Edition, Tinted Paper. 8vo, cloth, red edges, 2.50; cloth, gilt edges, 3.50.

THE STILL HOUR; or, Communion with God. By Prof. AUSTIN PHELPS, D. D., of Andover Theological Seminary. 16mo, cloth, 60 cts.

CHRISTIANITY AND STATESMANSHIP; with Kindred Topics. By WILLIAM HAGUE, D. D. A new, revised, enlarged, and much improved edition. 12mo, cloth, 1.75.

THE EVIDENCES OF CHRISTIANITY, as exhibited in the writings of its apologists, down to Augustine. By W. J. BOLTON, of Gonville and Caius College, Cambridge. 12mo, cloth, 1.50.

CHRISTIAN BROTHERHOOD. By BARON STOW, D. D., Pastor of Rowe-street Church, Boston. 16mo, cloth, 75 cts.

THE CHRISTIAN WORLD UNMASKED. By JOHN BERRIDGE, M., Vicar of Everton, Bedfordshire. With a Life of the Author, by Rev. THOMAS GUTHRIE, D. D., Minister of Free St. John's, Edinburgh. 16mo, cloth, 75 cts.

LIFE, TIMES, AND CORRESPONDENCE OF JAMES MANNING, AND THE EARLY HISTORY OF BROWN UNIVERSITY. By REUBEN ALDRIDGE GUILD. With Likenesses of President Manning and Nicholas Brown, Views of Brown University, The First Baptist Church, Providence, etc. Royal 12mo, cloth, 3.00.

A most important and interesting historical work.

MEMOIR OF GEORGE N. BRIGGS, LL. D., late Governor of Massachusetts. By W. C. RICHARDS. With Illustrations. Royal 12mo. 2.50

THE LIFE OF JOHN MILTON, narrated in connection with the POLITICAL, ECCLESIASTICAL, AND LITERARY HISTORY OF HIS TIME. By DAVID MASSON, M. A., Professor of English Literature, University College, London. Vol. I., embracing the period from 1608 to 1639. With Portraits and specimens of his handwriting at different periods. Royal octavo, cloth, 3.50.

LIFE AND CORRESPONDENCE OF REV. DANIEL WILSON, D. D., late Bishop of Calcutta. By Rev. JOSIAH BATEMAN, M. A., Rector of North Cray, Kent. With Portraits, Map, and numerous Illustrations. One volume royal octavo, cloth, 3.50.

☞ **An interesting life of a great and good man.**

THE LIFE AND TIMES OF JOHN HUSS; or, The Bohemian Reformation of the Fifteenth Century. By Rev. E. H. GILLETT. Two vols. royal octavo, 7.00.

"The author," says the *New York Observer*, "has achieved a great work, performed a valuable service for Protestantism and the world, made a name for himself among religious historians, and produced a book that will hold a prominent place in the esteem of every religious scholar."

The *New York Evangelist* speaks of it as "one of the most valuable contributions to ecclesiastical history yet made in this country."

MEMOIR OF THE CHRISTIAN LABORS, Pastoral and Philanthropic, of THOMAS CHALMERS, D. D. L. L. D. By FRANCIS WAYLAND 16mo, cloth, 1.00.

The moral and intellectual greatness of Chalmers is, we might say, overwhelming to the mind of the ordinary reader. Dr. Wayland draws the portraiture with a master hand. — Method. Quart. Rev.

LIFE OF JAMES MONTGOMERY. By Mrs. H. C. KNIGHT, author of "Lady Huntington and her Friends," etc. Likeness, and elegant Illustrated Title-Page on steel. 12mo, cloth, 1.50.

DIARY AND CORRESPONDENCE OF AMOS LAWRENCE. With a brief account of some Incidents in his Life. Edited by his son, WM. R. LAWRENCE, M. D. With elegant Portraits of Amos and Abbott Lawrence, an Engraving of their Birthplace, an Autograph page of Handwriting, and a copious Index. One large octavo volume, cloth, 2.50.

THE SAME WORK. Royal 12mo, cloth, 1.75.

DR. GRANT AND THE MOUNTAIN NESTORIANS. By Rev. THOMAS LAURIE, his surviving associate in that Mission. With a Likeness, Map of the Country, and numerous Illustrations. Third edition. Revised and improved. 12mo, cloth, 1.75. ☞ A most valuable memoir of a *remarkable man.*

HACKETT'S COMMENTARY ON THE ORIGINAL TEXT OF THE ACTS OF THE APOSTLES. By HORATIO B. HACKETT, D. D., Prof. of Biblical Literature and Interpretation in the Newton Theol. Institute. ☞ A new, revised, and enlarged edition. Royal octavo, cloth, 3.00.

☞ This most important and very popular work has been thoroughly revised; large portions entirely re-written, with the addition of *more than one hundred pages of new matter;* the result of the author's continued investigations and travels since the publication of the first edition.

HACKETT'S ILLUSTRATIONS OF SCRIPTURE. Suggested by a Tour through the Holy Land. With numerous Illustrations. A new, Improved, and Enlarged edition. By H. B. HACKETT, D. D., Prof. of Biblical Literature in the Newton Theol. Institution. 12mo, cloth, 1.50.

FINE EDITION, TINTED PAPER. Square 8vo, cloth, red edges, 2.50; cloth, gilt, 3.50; half calf, 5.00; full Turkey mor., 7.50.

Prof. Hackett's accuracy is proverbial. We can rely on his statements with confidence, which is in itself a pleasure. He knows and appreciates the wants of readers; explains the texts which need explanation; gives life-like pictures, and charms while he instructs. — *N. Y. Observer.*

MUSIC OF THE BIBLE; or, Explanatory Notes upon all the passages of the Sacred Scriptures relating to Music. With a brief Essay on Hebrew Poetry. By ENOCH HUTCHINSON. With numerous Illustrations. Royal octavo, 3.25.

This book is altogether a unique production, and will be found of interest not only to Biblical scholars and clergymen generally, but also to Sabbath-school teachers, musicians, and the family circle. It is illustrated with numerous engravings.

MALCOM'S NEW BIBLE DICTIONARY of the most important Names, Objects, and Terms found in the Holy Scriptures; intended principally for Sabbath-School Teachers and Bible Classes. By HOWARD MALCOM, D. D., late President of Lewisburg University, Pa. 16mo, cloth, 1.00.

☞ The former Dictionary, of which more than *one hundred thousand copies* were sold, is made the basis of the present work.

PATTISON'S COMMENTARY ON THE EPISTLE TO THE EPHESIANS, Explanatory, Doctrinal, and Practical. With a Series of Questions. By ROBERT E. PATTISON, D. D., late President of Waterville College. 12mo, cloth, 1.25.

RIPLEY'S NOTES ON THE GOSPELS. Designed for Teachers in Sabbath Schools and Bible Classes, and as an Aid to Family Instruction. By HENRY J. RIPLEY, Prof. in Newton Theol. Inst. With Map of Canaan. Cloth, embossed, 1.75.

RIPLEY'S NOTES ON THE ACTS OF THE APOSTLES. With a beautiful Map, illustrating the Travels of the APOSTLE PAUL, with a track of his Voyage from Cesarea to Rome. By Prof. HENRY J. RIPLEY, D. D. 12mo, cloth, embossed, 1.25

RIPLEY'S NOTES ON THE EPISTLE OF PAUL TO THE ROMANS. Designed for Teachers in Sabbath Schools and Bible Classes, and as an Aid to Family Instruction. By HENRY J. RIPLEY. 12mo, cloth, embossed, 90 cts.

The above works by Prof. Ripley should be in the hands of every student of the Bible, especially every Sabbath-school and Bible-class teacher. They contain just the kind of information wanted

CRUDEN'S CONDENSED CONCORDANCE. A Complete Concordance to the Holy Scriptures. By ALEXANDER CRUDEN. Revised and re-edited by the Rev. DAVID KING, LL. D. Octavo, cloth arabesque, 1.75; sheep, 2.00.

The condensation of the quotations of Scripture, arranged under the most obvious heads, while it *diminishes the bulk* of the work, *greatly facilitates* the finding of any required passage.
"We have in this edition of Cruden the *best* made *better*." — *Puritan Recorder.*

EADIE'S ANALYTICAL CONCORDANCE OF THE HOLY SCRIPTURES; or, the Bible presented under Distinct and Classified Heads or Topics. By JOHN EADIE, D. D. LL. D., Author of "Biblical Cyclopædia," "Ecclesiastical Cyclopædia," "Dictionary of the Bible," etc. One volume, octavo, 840 pp., cloth, 4.00; sheep, 5.00; cloth, gilt, 5.50; half calf, 6.50.

The object of this Concordance is to present the SCRIPTURES ENTIRE, under certain classified and exhaustive heads. It differs from an ordinary Concordance, in that its arrangement depends not on WORDS, but on SUBJECTS, and the verses *are printed in full.*

KITTO'S POPULAR CYCLOPÆDIA OF BIBLICAL LITERATURE. Condensed from the larger work. By the Author, JOHN KITTO, D. D. Assisted by JAMES TAYLOR, D. D., of Glasgow. With over five hundred Illustrations. One volume, octavo, 812 pp., cloth, 4.00; sheep, 5.00; half calf, 7.00.

A DICTIONARY OF THE BIBLE. Serving also as a COMMENTARY, embodying the products of the best and most recent researches in biblical literature in which the scholars of Europe and America have been engaged.

KITTO'S HISTORY OF PALESTINE, from the Patriarchal Age to the Present Time; with Chapters on the Geography and Natural History of the Country, the Customs and Institutions of the Hebrews. By JOHN KITTO, D. D. With upwards of two hundred Illustrations. 12mo, cloth, 1.75.

☞ A work admirably adapted to the Family, the Sabbath School, and the week-day School Library

WESTCOTT'S INTRODUCTION TO THE STUDY OF THE GOSPELS. With HISTORICAL AND EXPLANATORY NOTES. By BROOKE FOSS WESTCOTT, M. A., late Fellow of Trinity College, Cambridge. With an Introduction by Prof. H. B. HACKETT, D. D. Royal 12mo, cloth, 2.00.

☞ A masterly work by a master mind.

ELLICOTT'S LIFE OF CHRIST HISTORICALLY CONSIDERED. The Hulsean Lectures for 1859, with Notes Critical, Historical, and Explanatory. By C. J. ELLICOTT, B. D. Royal 12mo, cloth, 1.75.

☞ Admirable in spirit, and profound in argument.

RAWLINSON'S HISTORICAL EVIDENCES OF THE TRUTH OF THE SCRIPTURE RECORDS, STATED ANEW, with Special reference to the Doubts and Discoveries of Modern Times. In Eight Lectures, delivered in the Oxford University pulpit, at the Bampton Lecture for 1859. By GEO. RAWLINSON, M. A., Editor of the Histories of Herodotus. With the Copious NOTES TRANSLATED for the *American edition* by an accomplished scholar. 12mo, cloth, 1.75.

"The consummate learning, judgment, and general ability, displayed by Mr. Rawlinson in his edition of Herodotus, are exhibited in this work also." — *North-American.*

THE PILGRIM'S PROGRESS from this World to that which is to come. By JOHN BUNYAN. NEW AND BEAUTIFUL EDITION, *with forty elegant Illustrations*, drawn by John Gilbert, and engraved by W. H. Whymper. Square 8vo, tinted paper, cloth, full gilt, 3.50; Turkey mor., 7.00.

CHRISTIAN MEMORIALS OF THE WAR. Embracing Scenes and Incidents of Christian Bravery and Religious Faith in the Army. With Historical Notes. By Prof. HORATIO B. HACKETT, D. D. 12mo, cloth, 1.50

TWEEDIE'S GLAD TIDINGS; or, The Gospel of Peace. A series of Daily Meditations for Christian Disciples. By Rev. W. K. TWEEDIE, D. D. With an elegant illustrated title-page. 16mo, cloth, 1.00; cloth, gilt, 1.50.

TWEEDIE'S LAMP TO THE PATH; or, the Bible in the Heart, the Home, and the Market-place. With an elegant illustrated title-page. 16mo, cloth, 1.00; cloth, gilt, 1.50.

TWEEDIE'S SEED-TIME AND HARVEST; or, Sow Well and Reap Well. A Book for the Young. With an elegant illustrated title-page. 16mo, cloth, 1.00; cloth, gilt, 1.50.

☞ The above interesting works, by Dr. Tweedie, are of uniform size and style, and well adapted for "gift books."

THE NEW ENGLAND THEOCRACY. From the German of Uhden's History of the Congregationalists of New England, with an INTRODUCTION BY NEANDER. By Mrs. H. C. CONANT, author of "The English Bible," etc. 12mo, cloth, 1.25.

A work of rare ability and interest, presenting the early religious and ecclesiastical history of New England, from authentic sources, with singular impartiality.

REPUBLICAN CHRISTIANITY; or, True Liberty, as exhibited in the Life, Precepts, and Early Disciples of the Great Redeemer. By the Rev. E. L. MAGOON, D. D. 12mo, cloth, 1.50.

SACRED RHETORIC; or, Composition and Delivery of Sermons. By H. J. RIPLEY, D. D., Prof. in Newton Theol. Inst. To which is added, DR. WARE'S HINTS ON EXTEMPORANEOUS PREACHING. 12mo, cloth, 1.25.

GUIDO AND JULIUS. THE DOCTRINE OF SIN AND THE PROPITIATOR; or The True Consecration of the Doubter. Exhibited in the Correspondence of two Friends. By FREDERICK AUGUSTUS O. THOLUCK, D. D. Translated from the German, by JONATHAN EDWARDS RYLAND. With an Introduction by JOHN PYE SMITH, D. D. 16mo, cloth, 75 cts.

SERVICE THE END OF LIVING. By ANDREW L. STONE, Pastor of Park-street Church, Boston. 16mo, paper covers, 20 cts.; flexible cloth, 35 cts.

☞ An admirable work for circulation, especially among young men.

THE SIGNET RING, AND OTHER GEMS. From the Dutch of Rev. J. DE LIEFDE. 16mo, cloth, 1.00.

☞ Seldom within so small a compass has such weighty teaching been presented with such exquisite and charming skill.

SIGNET RING AND ITS HEAVENLY MOTTO. From the Dutch of Rev. J. DE LIEFDE. 16mo, cloth, flexible, gilt edges, 50 cts.

WILLIAMS'S LECTURES ON THE LORD'S PRAYER. By WILLIAM R. WILLIAMS, D. D. Third edition, 12mo, cloth, 1.25.

"We are constantly reminded, in reading his eloquent pages, of the old English writers, whose vigorous thought, and gorgeous imagery, and varied learning, have made their writings an inexhaustible mine for the scholars of the present day." — *Ch. Observer.*

WILLIAMS'S MISCELLANIES. By WILLIAM R. WILLIAMS, D. D. New and improved edition. 12mo, cloth, 1.75.

"Dr. Williams is a profound scholar and a brilliant writer." — *N. Y. Evangelist.*

WILLIAMS'S RELIGIOUS PROGRESS; Discourses on the Development of the Christian Character. By WILLIAM R. WILLIAMS, D. D. Third edition, 12mo, cloth, 1.25.

"His power of apt and forcible illustration is without a parallel among modern writers. The mute pages spring into life beneath the magic of his radiant imagination. But this is never at the expense of solidity of thought, or strength of argument. It is seldom, indeed, that a mind of so much poetical invention yields such a willing homage to the logical element." — *Harper's Monthly Miscellany.*

HARRIS'S GREAT TEACHER; or, Characteristics of our Lord's Ministry. By JOHN HARRIS, D. D. With an Introductory Essay by H. HUMPHREY, D. D. Sixteenth thousand. 12mo, cloth, 1.50.

"Dr. HARRIS is one of the best writers of the age; and this volume will not in the least detract from his well-merited reputation." — *American Pulpit.*

HARRIS'S GREAT COMMISSION; or, The Christian Church constituted and charged to convey the Gospel to the World. A Prize Essay. With an Introductory Essay by W. R. WILLIAMS, D. D. Eighth thousand. 12mo, cloth, 1.75.

"This volume will afford the reader an intellectual and spiritual banquet of the highest order." — *Philadelphia Ch. Observer.*

HARRIS'S MAN PRIMEVAL; or, The Constitution and Primitive Condition of the Human Being. With a finely-engraved Portrait of the Author. 12mo, cloth, 1.50.

"His copious and beautiful illustrations of the successive laws of the Divine Manifestation have yielded us inexpressible delight." — *London Eclectic Review.*

HARRIS'S PRE-ADAMITE EARTH. Contributions to Theological Science. By JOHN HARRIS, D. D. New and revised edition. 12mo, cloth, 1.50.

"We have never seen the natural sciences, particularly geology, made to give so decided and unimpeachable testimony to revealed truth." — *Christian Mirror.*

HARRIS'S PATRIARCHY; or, The Family, its Constitution and Probation. 12mo, cloth, 1.75.

This is the last of Dr. Harris's valuable series entitled "Contributions to Theological Science."

HARRIS'S SERMONS, CHARGES, ADDRESSES, etc., delivered by Dr. HARRIS in various parts of the country, during the height of his reputation as a preacher. Two elegant volumes, octavo, cloth, each 1.50.

The immense sale of all this author's works attests their intrinsic worth and great popularity.

WAYLAND'S LETTERS ON THE MINISTRY OF THE GOSPEL. By FRANCIS WAYLAND, D.D. 16mo, cloth, 90 cts.

WAYLAND'S SALVATION BY CHRIST. A Series of Discourses on some of the most Important Doctrines of the Gospel. By FRANCIS WAYLAND, D.D. 12mo, cloth, 1.50; cloth, gilt, 2.25.

THE LIFE OF TRUST; being a Narrative of the Dealings of God with the REV. GEORGE MÜLLER. Edited and condensed by Rev. H. LINCOLN WAYLAND. With an Introduction by FRANCIS WAYLAND, D.D. Cloth, 1.75.

This work has a peculiar charm, as an unadorned story of the experience of a Christian man who believed in the mighty power of prayer, who gave a literal interpretation to the precept, "Take no thought for the morrow," and lived by daily faith in God's providence and grace.

THE YEAR OF GRACE: a History of the Great Revival in Ireland in 1859. By Rev. WILLIAM GIBSON, Professor of Christian Ethics in the Presbyterian College, Belfast. 12mo, cloth, 1.75.

A remarkable book on a remarkable subject. Next to a visit to the scenes of the Revival, nothing can give so adequate an idea of the wonderful work as the thrilling narrative of Prof. Gibson.

MEMORIALS OF EARLY CHRISTIANITY; Presenting, in a graphic, compact, and popular form, Memorable Events of Early Ecclesiastical History, etc. By Rev. J. G. MIALL, author of "Footsteps of our Forefathers." With numerous Illustrations. 12mo, cloth, 1.50.

FOOTSTEPS OF OUR FOREFATHERS; What they Suffered and what they Sought. Describing Localities, and Portraying Personages and Events, conspicuous in the Struggles for Religious Liberty. By JAMES G. MIALL. Containing thirty-six Illustrations. 12mo, cloth, 1.50.

MODERN ATHEISM; Under its forms of Pantheism, Materialism, Secularism, Development, and Natural Laws. By JAMES BUCHANAN, D. D., LL. D. 12mo, cloth, 1.75.

"The work is one of the most readable and solid which we have ever perused." — *Hugh Miller.*

MORNING HOURS IN PATMOS. The Opening Vision of the Apocalypse, and Christ's Epistle to the Seven Churches of Asia. By Rev. A. C. THOMPSON, D. D., author of "The Better Land," "Gathered Lilies," etc. With beautiful Frontispiece. 12mo, cloth, 1.50.

FIRST THINGS; or, the Development of Church Life. By BARON STOW, D. D. 16mo, cloth, 90 cts.

THE GREAT CONCERN; or, Man's Relation to God and a Future State. By NEHEMIAH ADAMS, D. D. 12mo, cloth, 1.25.

"Pungent and affectionate, reaching the intellect, conscience, and feelings; admirably fitted to awaken, guide, and instruct. Just the thing for distribution in our congregations." —*N. Y. Observer.*

EVENINGS WITH THE DOCTRINES. By Rev. NEHEMIAH ADAMS, D. D. Royal 12mo, cloth, 1.75.

TRUTHS FOR THE TIMES. By NEHEMIAH ADAMS, D. D., Pastor of Essex-street Church, Boston. 12mo, paper covers, 15 and 30 cts.

www.ingramcontent.com/pod-product-compliance
Lightning Source LLC
LaVergne TN
LVHW010226110826
845151LV00004B/1194
9781425526672